AFTA SpringerBriefs in Family Therapy

For further volumes:
http://www.springer.com/series/11846

Thorana Nelson • Hinda Winawer
Editors

Critical Topics in Family Therapy

AFTA Monograph Series Highlights

Springer

Editors
Thorana Nelson
Santa Fe
New Mexico
USA

Hinda Winawer
Princeton
New Jersey
USA

ISSN 2196-5528 ISSN 2196-5536 (electronic)
ISBN 978-3-319-03247-4 ISBN 978-3-319-03248-1 (eBook)
DOI 10.1007/978-3-319-03248-1
Springer Cham Heidelberg New York Dordrecht London

Library of Congress Control Number: 2013955746

Printed on acid-free paper

Springer is part of Springer Science+Business Media (www.springer.com)

To AFTA, a unique organization that integrates social justice in contexts of mental health practice: we dedicate this volume with gratitude.

Acknowledgements

The essence of this volume was conceptualized, executed, fine-tuned, and celebrated long before *Critical Topics in Family Therapy: AFTA Monograph Series Highlights* was compiled. The chapters in this book were originated from essays in former American Family Therapy Academy (AFTA) Monographs, published between 2005 and 2011 and available to AFTA members. This volume introduces the AFTA SpringerBriefs in Family Therapy series, and the Academy's future work will be available to a broader audience through a collaboration between AFTA and Springer.

First, great thanks are due to the diligence and foundational work of the Editors-in-Chief of the Monographs: Betty MacKune-Karrer (2005), Laura Roberto-Foreman (2005–2010), and Melissa Elliott (2011). We appreciate your perseverance and dedication to the publications, to the Guest Editors, and to AFTA. Working in collaboration with Guest Editors, you oversaw selection of themes, were consulted regarding contributions, and provided both editorial and administrative support for production from text to artwork to distribution. Thank you, Betty, Melissa, and Laura.

To the Guest Editors of the Monographs that are represented here—Jodie KIiman, Ramón Rojano, John Sargent, Martha Edwards, Jane Ariel, Pilar Hernandez-Wolfe, Sarah Stearns, Arlene Lev, and Jean Malpas—we cannot thank you enough for the work you did on the Monographs you edited. The inception of each monograph, from idea through invitation of authors, involved much thought and consultation with the Editors-in-Chief, the AFTA board and other members, and prospective authors. Each of you sought out scholars who were on the cutting edge of your subject area, supported their work in whatever way was necessary, and introduced it with respect and admiration.

To each of the Contributors, we thank you for your permission to adapt these articles for this first AFTA/SpringerScience publication and of course, we acknowledge and value the significance of your work. Each of you brought special perspectives and expertise to the subject matter and to your contribution. These articles are now the meat of a new AFTA publication.

To AFTA members who read these works, to the Board of Directors that has approved this publication, and to Jennifer Hadley at Springer who helped develop this project, thank you. We also would like to acknowledge the two administrators at the helm and the heart of AFTA, former Director Barbro Miles and current Director, Kim Cox, for your behind-the-scenes ferrying of all these works through to production.

To Hinda Winawer, I, Thorana, thank you for your persistence and continual dedication to making this project work. I believe this volume and the forthcoming AFTA SpringerScience Briefs volumes will be great contributions to the integration of social context into mental health philosophies and practice.

To Thorana Nelson, I, Hinda, thank you for your leadership in seeing this project through from idea to press, and for your collaboration in the groundwork of creating AFTA SpringerScience Briefs. Without your experience, diligence, and patience, we could not have accomplished this project for AFTA.

Thorana Nelson
Santa Fe

Hinda Winawer
Princeton

Editorial Acknowledgements

Editors of this Volume

Thorana S. Nelson PhD

Hinda Winawer MSW, LCSW (AFTA President 2011–2013)

The following served as AFTA Publications Chairs and Editors-in-Chief of the AFTA Monograph Series. Their dedication to their task is evident in the quality of the monographs.

Betty MacKune-Karrer MSW (2005)

Laura Roberto-Forman PsyD (2005–2010)

Melissa Elliott MSN (2011)

The following served as guest editors for the Monographs. We credit the excellence of the Monographs Series to their careful guidance.

Jodie Kliman PhD, Touched by War Zones, Near and Far: Oscillations of Despair and Hope, 2005

Ramón Rojano MD, Lessons Learned in Community Practice, 2005

John Sargent MD, Systemic Responses to Disaster: Stories of the Aftermath of Hurricane Katrina, 2007

Martha Edwards PhD, Neuroscience and Family Therapy: Integrations and Applications, 2008

Jane Ariel PhD, **Pilar Hernandez-Wolfe** PhD, and **Sarah Stearns** PhD, Expanding Our Social Justice Practices: Advances in Theory and Training, 2010

Arlene Lev MSW, LCSW, CASAC and **Jean Malpas** MA, DES, LMHC, LMFT At the Edge: Exploring Gender and Sexuality in Couples and Families, 2011

Contents

Contributors

Daisy Barros is a School Counselor and Couple and Family Therapist with Fundación Nuestra Casa (Our Home) in Barranquilla, Colombia.

Ellen I. Bassuk MD, is Founder, Center of Social Innovation, Needham, MA; Founder and former President, the National Center on Family Homelessness; and Associate Professor of Psychiatry, Harvard Medical School, Boston, MA.

Ćielo de Cure is a Social Worker and Family and Couple Therapist with Fundación Nuestra Casa (Our Home), Barranquilla, Colombia.

Silvia de Navarro is a Social Worker and Couple and Family Therapist with Fundación Nuestra Casa (Our Home) in Barranquilla, Colombia.

Katia de Rosales is a Clinical Psychologist and Couple and Family Therapist with Fundación Nuestra Casa (Our Home) in Barranquilla, Colombia.

Maria Teresa de Sabbagh is a Clinical Psychologist and Family and Couple Therapist with Fundación Nuestra Casa (Our Home) in Barranquilla, Colombia.

Carmen Maria de Salazar is a School Counselor and Couple and Family Therapist with Fundación Nuestra Casa (Our Home) in Barranquilla, Colombia.

Maria de Theran is a Clinical Psychologist and Couple and Family Therapist with Fundación Nuestra Casa (Our Home) in Barranquilla, Colombia.

Deanna M. Fierman MA, currently works in private practice and at the University of Colorado Boulder in Boulder, Colorado.

Mona DeKoven Fishbane PhD, is a clinical psychologist in private practice in Chicago and Highland Park, IL and is director of couple therapy training at the Chicago Center for Family Health Chicago, IL.

Peter Fraenkel, PhD, is an associate professor of clinical psychology at the City University of New York and Director of the Center for Work and Family at the Ackerman Institute for the Family, New York, NY.

James Garrett MSW, LCSW-R, CAI, BRI- II, is Co-Founder of ARISE and Founding Director of the Recovery Resource Center, Albany, NY.

Yael Geron PhD, is Clinical Associate Professor and head of the School of Social Work at Zefat Academic College, Zefat, Israel.

Shawn V. Giammattei PhD, is the coordinator of training for the Rockway Institute, a faculty member at the California School of Professional Psychology at Alliant International University, and a Clinical/Research Associate of the Child and Adolescent Gender Center at UCSF. He also is in private practice in San Francisco and Santa Rosa, CA.

Marissa Gold-Peifer PsyD, is a licensed psychologist in private practice in Boston, MA.

Jaqueline Hudak PhD, is the Clinical Director for the Center for Couples and Adult Families, Department of Psychiatry, Perlman School of Medicine, University of Pennsylvania, Philadelphia, PA. She also is in private practice in NJ.

Madhubala Ishver Kasiram PhD, is Professor of Social Work in the School of Applied Human Sciences at the University of KwaZulu Natal in Durban, South Africa and is in private practice in Durban, South Africa.

Kristina Konnath MSW, LICSW, is the Co-Director of the Pathways to Permanency Program at the Justice Resource Institute (JRI) in Boston, MA, providing supervisory and clinical services through JRI's outpatient clinics, The Trauma Center and Metrowest Behavioral Health Center.

Judith Landau MD, DPM, LMFT, CFLE, CAI, BRI II, CIP, is a child, family and community psychiatrist and ARISE Co-Founder, CEO and President of Linking Human Systems, LLC and LINC Foundation, Inc, Boulder, CO.

Roxana Llerena-Quinn PhD, is a psychologist in the Department of Outpatient Psychiatry at Boston Children's Hospital, Harvard Medical School, Boston, MA.

Rosa Maria Stefanini de Macedo PhD, is Professor Emerita at Pontifical Catholic University of São Paulo, Brazil; Coordinator of the Nucleus of Studies and Research in Family and Community at the Graduate Program of Clinical Psychology; and Family and Couple Therapist in private practice at Sao Paulo, Brazil.

Melissa MacNish MA, LMHC, is a licensed mental health counselor in private practice in Boston, MA.

Ruth Malkinson PhD, is with the International Center for the Study of Loss, Bereavement, and Human Resilience, University of Haifa, Israel. She is also in private practice in Haifa.

Beatriz Maria Molina Velez MSW, was a private practitioner and retired Professor with Universidad Pontificia Bolivariana, Medellin, Colombia.

Margaret Nichols PhD, is the Executive Director of the Institute for Personal Growth in NJ.

Emmerentie Oliphant PhD, is Professor and Director of the MSW Program at the Stephen F. Austin State University in Nacogdoches, Texas.

Marcelo Pakman MD, is a community psychiatrist, family therapist, and international lecturer, Springfield, MA.

Esther Perel MA, LMFT, serves on the faculties of the Family Studies Unit of the Department of Psychiatry, New York University Medical Center; the American Association for Sex Educators and Therapists; the International Trauma Studies Program of the Ackerman Institute for the Family; and the Scandinavian Institute for Expressive Arts Therapies.

Shruti Singh Poulsen PhD, is an assistant professor at the University of Colorado Denver in the Counseling program and is in clinical practice as a couple and family therapist, Denver, CO.

Jelisaveta Sanja Rolovic PhD, is a clinical psychologist and marriage and family therapist with a private practice in New York, NY.

Michal Shamai PhD, is Associate Professor at the University of Haifa, School of Social Work in Haifa, Israel. She also is head of Family Studies at the School of Social Work Master's program and is on the staff of the Center of Research and Family Studies at the University of Haifa.

Katherine T. Volk MA, is the Managing Director of t3 (think. teach. transform.) and a Senior Associate at the Center for Social Innovation in Needham, MA.

[illegible] Professor [illegible] Director of the MSW Program [illegible]

[illegible] Springfield, MA

[illegible]

[illegible]

Critical Topics in Family Therapy: AFTA Monograph Series Highlights

Thorana Nelson and Hinda Winawer

Introduction

With this volume, the American Family Therapy Academy (AFTA) introduces the AFTA SpringerScience Briefs Series. The current offering is a special edition drawn from articles in the previously published AFTA Monograph Series and will be followed by stand-alone, thematic volumes in the Briefs series. Contributions to the current volume were authored by experts in the field of family therapy and reflect core aspects of AFTA: systemic and post-modern thinking, and AFTA's commitment to social justice in the culture of the organization, in clinical inquiry, and in training. Psychotherapists, academics, and clinical teachers will find these works inspiring and provocative; they are firmly rooted in the history of conversations about the evolution of family therapy within AFTA. Through collaboration with SpringerScience, AFTA now is able to offer the special expertise of AFTA to a worldwide audience.

This Volume and the Legacy of AFTA

Many of the chapters selected for this special edition exemplify collaborative thinking and practice in contexts that are oppressive due to often co-occurring environmental factors. Although the overall AFTA Monograph Series illustrates the evolution of the integration of social justice and clinical practice, we selected the particular chapters in this volume because they highlight recent cutting edge developments that addressed clinical challenges in adverse social contexts. We also

T. Nelson (✉)
Santa Fe, NM, USA
e-mail: thorana.nelson@usu.edu

H. Winawer
Princeton, NJ, USA
e-mail: hindawinawer@cfcsj.net

T. Nelson, H. Winawer (eds.), *Critical Topics in Family Therapy*,
AFTA SpringerBriefs in Family Therapy, DOI 10.1007/978-3-319-03248-1_1,

feature another recent integrative initiative: the linking of principles of neuroscience with family systems concepts and practice. Contributors addressing work in adverse social contexts demonstrate theory and practice that is informed by the significance of power and privilege in psychotherapy, in program development, and in clinical training. Authors discuss their feelings as well as clinical dilemmas. They address salient phenomena that are often relegated to the margins of dominant discourse or to invisibility within that discourse in our society and in the mental health fields: expanding the boundaries of sexual pleasure, sexual orientation, and gender identity; the dominance of heteronormative thinking; homelessness; dealing with "enemies" in war-torn countries; the impact of natural disaster on children and families; and the ongoing oppression of living in poor, violent communities. This volume brings these aspects of the human condition and the people who survive them to the center of therapeutic discourse.

The articles related to neuroscience address the relationship of brain functioning to family and couple communication and to understanding addiction. Too often, such science is used to suggest that individual, couple, and family functioning are not important aspects of a complex functioning that includes individuals' biology—the medical model which suggests that brain anomalies *cause* emotional and behavioral suffering. These chapters add a perspective beyond this causal, linear paradigm in their inclusion of relational aspects of neuroscience.

AFTA: A Brief Retrospective. The American Family Therapy Academy was founded in 1977 by leading family therapists and has fostered collegial exchange to expand the context of mental health and family systems inquiry, understanding, and healing in psychotherapy. At the time of its first annual meeting in 1979, a family systems perspective was emerging throughout the United States and in other countries. System thinking (von Bertalanffy 1968) incorporates assumptions and a paradigm of understanding human thinking, emotions, and behavior as influenced by and influencing all realms of existence—an ecological perspective that suggests that everything exists within contexts. These contexts mutually influence each other although some exert more influence than others. In addition, changes in one part of a system reverberate throughout the entire system of contexts, requiring adaptation and further change. These systems and their interactions among each other then become the focus of understanding human behavior and clinical work. As an organization, AFTA is dedicated to building positive systemic change for clients, individuals, and families in general, as well as for both local and global communities.

The AFTA founders were an interdisciplinary group of established psychiatrists, clinical social workers, couples and family therapists, and psychologists. They became outliers in their own disciplines because they introduced a paradigm shift from focus on the individual to relationships. Ideas were considered so revolutionary that the first AFTA president (Murray Bowen) delivered a paper at a national conference of family researchers in 1967 about his own family of origin, which he then published, authored as "Anonymous" (found in Framo 1972). These ideas expanded the boundaries of the European individually oriented psychoanalytic perspective, which had been the exclusive lens for examination of human behavior. In addition to system thinking, cybernetics (Weiner 1948), and the cutting edge relational perspective of anthropologist Gregory Bateson (e.g., 1972) were core concepts.

Social change within society was gradually mirrored in AFTA's membership, leadership, and in the focus of clinical work and scholarship. Feminism, multiculturalism, and sexual and gender identity and orientation provided additional dimensions of complexity to clinical investigation and intervention. Systemic thinking began to incorporate postmodern perspectives, which shifted the focus of inquiry to meaning in the individual, family, and social context. Linear thinking, exclusively medically based models, and a modernist quest for objective truth were replaced with clinical inquiry that privileged the knowledge of the client, valued transparency and resilience, and explored meaning as embedded in social contexts. AFTA became a setting for exploring and developing approaches to treatment, research, and training that were collaborative and relevant to the ethnic cultures and contexts of our clients.

The prevalence of oppression and marginalization in society compels us to develop new approaches to clinical work and teaching, and to apply our knowledge as psychotherapists to influence policies that affect the health and well-being of children and families (see www.afta.org for AFTA position papers). As AFTA members became increasingly aware of the negative impacts of oppressive contexts and discourse on individuals, couples, families, and communities, they began to influence the discourse in both public and private ways. These included presentations and discussion groups at AFTA annual meetings, which were then reported on and reflected in AFTA publications.

The Evolution of AFTA Publications

Previous formats of AFTA authoring included the former internal publication, the *AFTA Newsletter*; the first commercial publication under the auspices of AFTA, *The Global Family Therapist: Integrating the Personal, Professional, and Political* (Berger-Gould and DeMuth 1994); and the AFTA Monograph series. Beginning in 2005, committed to social justice, clinical and research innovation, and sharing of ideas, AFTA decided to publish collections of essays and articles as standalone publications rather than embedded in the *Newsletter*. The collections centered on topics that affect families in the realms of policy and health care, particularly mental health, and in the context of systemic family therapy to spread the wealth of information and expertise that AFTA members could share with each other and others. The first monograph (2005) focused on war and the effects of war, including its impact on children. This monograph was quickly followed by others on topics focusing on community practice (2005), immigration (2006), natural disaster (2007), and neuroscience, leading and not merely following innovative clinical work and social discourse.

In addition to the current special edition, future AFTA collections will be available globally as part of the SpringerScience Briefs series. These volumes will be collections that are unique and constructed by AFTA. The AFTA SpringerScience Briefs will now be the most public version of written exchanges about systemic clinical theory, research, and practice within AFTA.

The Current Work

We selected articles from the Monographs that reflect the values and mission of AFTA and that also present high possibilities for academic reading, teaching, clinical work, and policy making. We did not select articles that were primarily personal reflections or responses to other articles. Each chosen article suggests a clinical as well as theoretical or philosophical perspective on the topic and is written in academic form. Many report on the development of systemic responses to difficult situations. We offer these as examples of programs that others may use in developing their own responses.

If your ideas are sparked by any of the chapters in this volume, we invite you to join the AFTA conversation. Attend AFTA's next Annual Meeting and Conference. You may want to submit a proposal for a brief presentation.

So, now, read on, allow yourself to think about what the authors are saying and the contexts in which they wrote. If you are a clinician, we hope that these chapters will provide information that will enhance your practice.

References

Anonymous. (1972). Toward a differentiation of self in one's own family. In J. Framo (Ed.), *Family interaction* (pp. 111–173). New York, NY: Springer.

Bateson, G. (1972). *Steps to an ecology of mind.* New York, NY: Ballantine Books.

Berger-Gould, B., & DeMuth, D. H. (1994). *The global family therapist: Integrating the personal, professional, and political.* Boston, MA: Allyn & Bacon.

von Bertalanffy, L. (1968). *General system theory: Foundations, development, applications*. New York, NY: Norton.

Weiner, N. (1948). *Cybernetics, or communication and control in the animal and the machine.* Cambridge, MA: MIT Press.

Part I

Touched by War Zones, Near and Far: Oscillations of Despair and Hope, 2005

—Jodie Kliman, Guest Editor

Families in the War Zone: Narratives of "Me" and the "Other" in the Course of Therapy

Yael Geron, Ruth Malkinson and Michal Shamai

Introduction

In this article, we will share some of our experiences of living with ongoing political conflict under a continuous threat to our lives. The point of view expressed reflects our effort to present our own overall perspective in relation to an absent "other." The current situation in Israeli society in a time of conflict with the Palestinians is analogous to that of a large family whose members tell many different stories and have many voices.

These stories and voices evolve; they change their volume, frequency, and heroes in relation to sociopolitical changes. These changes can be viewed from the perspective of the social construction of meaning. The many voices form a variety of narratives of "me" and of the "other" (the enemy), the auditory equivalent of looking through a kaleidoscope. The major factors that shape collective and subjective construction of meaning have political, economic, social, religious, and personal components, all of which create multiple narratives in relation to each other. We will elaborate on each of these aspects from the perspective of the Israeli narratives, but assume, based on our experience, that Palestinian narratives are not dissimilar. Although these factors are related, we will focus on each one separately to illustrate how each is perceived by representatives of both sides of the continuum.

Editors' note: First published in 2005, American Family Therapy Academy Monograph Series.

Y. Geron (✉)
Zefat Academic College, Zefat, Israel
e-mail: geron@post.tau.ac.il

R. Malkinson
Center for the Study of Loss, Bereavement, and Human Resilience,
University of Haifa, Haifa, Israel

M. Shamai
School of Social Work, University of Haifa, Haifa, Israel

T. Nelson, H. Winawer (eds.), *Critical Topics in Family Therapy*,
AFTA SpringerBriefs in Family Therapy, DOI 10.1007/978-3-319-03248-1_2,

Political Factors

The narratives of the extreme "left" and the "right" ideologies, although similar, are influential at opposite extremes of the political continuum. The essence of the narrative on the left is that of "peace and coexistence," in which the "other" is perceived as a partner. The essence of the narrative on the right is "peace and security," in which thc "other" is perceived as an enemy.

Economic Factors

Economic narratives also include two poles. On the one hand, conflict is seen as weakening Israeli economic growth, whereas on the other pole, the state of the economy is not seen as related to the conflict. For instance, some Israelis view the employment of Palestinians in Israel as contributing to Israel's national economic growth in specific fields, such as building construction. This perspective acknowledges a mutual accommodation of each group to the "other." At the other extreme is the perception among Israelis that Palestinians' employment damages the Israeli economy. From the latter perspective, Palestinians are seen as causing damage by competing with Israeli workers, which results in an increased unemployment rate in Israel. In this narrative, the other is perceived as an enemy.

Social Factors

Social factors include the effects of the conflict on social unity and on welfare policy. Throughout the years, there have been changes in Israel's welfare policy. A few decades ago, welfare policy received priority, but with the growing expenses of national security costs, welfare and education policy have suffered great cuts in financial resources delivered to families and individuals, as well as in social security allowances.

Religious Factors

From the traditional perspective of Jewish religious beliefs, settling in the Bible's "promised land" is a spiritual commandment (*mitzva*). From that perspective, the "other," who is also in the "promised land," is considered an enemy who disturbs the fulfillment of this *mitzva*. From a moderate religious perspective and a secular one, the above idea is considered unjust because it is inhuman to deport people from their houses and land. The "other" is perceived as equal to oneself. In Israel there exists a linkage between organized religion and national-political issues, for example, in family, marital, and divorce laws. Presently, this linkage increases with the involvement of religious parties in the governmental coalition. Needless to say, religious beliefs and political ideologies are linked in the Israeli reality.

Personal Components

Under continuous stress, as is the case nowadays in Israel, reactivation of past traumatic personal experiences are not uncommon; it is frequently seen among Holocaust survivors, families bereaved as a result of wars and terrorist attacks, soldiers and civilians suffering from PTSD, and so forth. These experiences affect the way the "other" is perceived. Representations of the "other" range from perceptions as an enemy to someone with whom to identify. It is beyond the scope of this paper to describe in full all the possible configurations of all the above elements. We therefore focus our discussion on the following issues: living in a war zone, the cycle of violence, and the effects of both on professional aspects of experience. Additionally, we will provide some illustrations of coexistence of "me" and the "other" by adopting a meta-prism through which we can look and touch on, at least in part, a sensitive and complicated ever-evolving narrative.

Living in a War Zone

Epidemiological studies carried out by Bliech, Gelkopf, and Solomon (2003) among 512 Israeli adults indicate that almost 50 % of the respondents had been exposed either directly or indirectly to terrorist attacks. However, only a very small percentage (9 %) showed symptoms of PTSD. Sixty percent felt their lives were in danger and 68 % felt their families and/or acquaintances were in danger. Yet, strikingly, 82 % felt optimistic about their personal future and 67 % felt optimistic about the future of the state of Israel.

The Cycle of Violence

It is possible to explain the dynamic between the Israelis and the Palestinians according to Melanie Klein's (1975) theory of the personal tendency to express aggression as a way of self-defense. Although Klein described this process as an intrapsychic phenomenon, others (e.g., Scharff and Scharff 1987) have applied her conceptualization to interpersonal relations. We take her conceptualization further, conceiving of it as a social process in which the subject symbolizes the "I/We" and the object symbolizes the "Other." As the cycle of violence proceeds, each subject in a conflictual interaction turns the "other" into a demon (See Fig. 1).

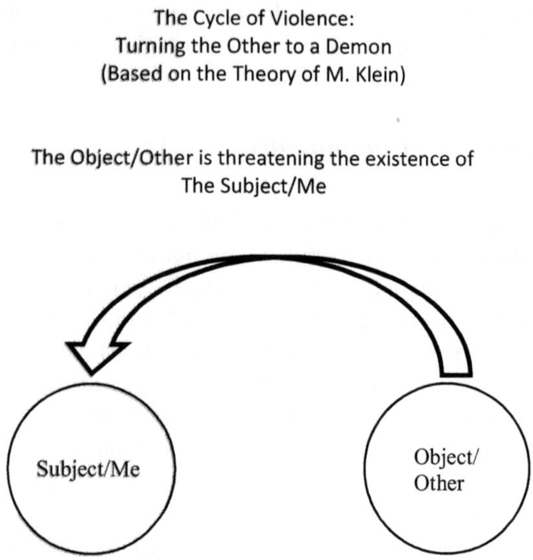

Fig. 1 The Cycle of Violence

In the cycle of violence:

- The Subject (I/We) experiences the "Other" (them) as threatening his or her existence and therefore as bad and dangerous.
- The Subject acts in an aggressive manner, which the Subject but not the Other perceives as self-defense.
- The Other perceives the Subject (Me/Us) as bad and dangerous.
- The Other attacks the Subject (Me/Us) in order to protect him/herself/themselves.
- As a result of the aggressive attacks, both the Subject and the Other are afraid of each other's revenge, thus the anxiety of both the Subject and Other increases.
- The Other (who is also his/her own Subject) perceives the Subject (who is also Other) as more dangerous and cruel—a demon.
- The cycle recursively continues.

The Subject and Object positions are, of course, interchangeable for both Israelis and Palestinians. The results of the cycle of violence can be illustrated as axes along two continua in which one axis represents the level of threat and the other represents the oscillation between humanization and demonization (see Fig. 2). The level of threat is positively associated with the humanization/demonization axis: As the level of threat increases, the tendency to demonize the other increases.

The Therapeutic Context

Since the entire population of Israel shares a common context of war and terror, both therapists and families are "in the same boat," with shared experiences of fear, anxiety, pain, and loss. The factors that affect the therapist's reactions might be

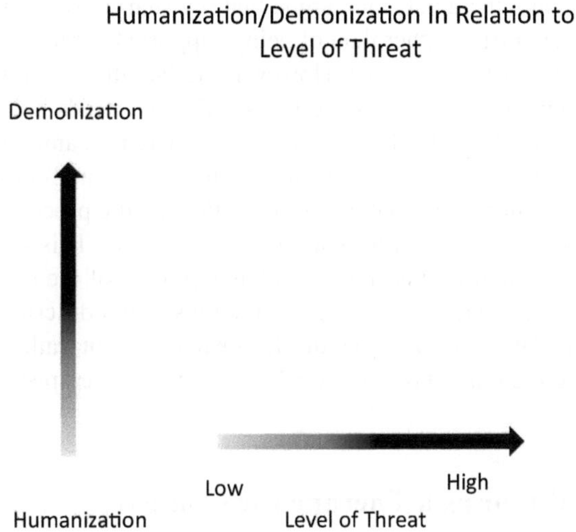

Fig. 2 The therapist fluctuates on both axes up and down due to continual threat situation

- The level of exposure, either direct or indirect, to the trauma of war and terror as happens when the therapist is at or near the terror event, or a relative or a friend is exposed to the event (Malkinson et al. 2005).
- The extent to which the therapeutic context, including the client's system, exposes the therapist to clinical material that relates to war and terror
- The extent to which the therapist's "routine" of the accumulated stress that results from living under continuous threat combines with the therapist's need to contain the stress of the client's system.
- The extent of the therapist's future orientation despite living with uncertainty and the continuous search for coping.

We illustrate the level of direct or indirect exposure with the following case example from one of our (MS) practices. Michal relates:

> Ori, as we will call him, has been in therapy for about two years. His son serves in the same army unit as my son. In one session, Ori told me that his son had informed him that he was going to Gaza, which was a particularly dangerous place at that time because of heavy fighting between the Israeli soldiers and the Palestinians. As Ori told his story, I became anxious and could not listen to him, even though I (unlike Ori) already knew the end of the story: the unit had not entered Gaza. I interrupted Ori's story and told him what I knew. He looked surprised and asked how I knew. I replied that I had gotten the same information from my son, adding that our sons serve in the same unit.
>
> For a few minutes, we talked about the army and about my experiences as the parent of a son in this unit. Moments later, as I realized the extent of my personal exposure in the therapeutic relationship, I felt defenseless as a result of over-identifying with Ori and therefore becoming the focus of therapy. In the following session, I asked Ori how he felt about my having taken his therapy time to share my own experiences as the parent of a soldier. Ori responded that he had been thinking about it during the week and had felt that he should have been more supportive of me, since I had been supportive of him during the entire process of therapy.

Some therapists may argue that my sharing with Ori gave him the option of being supportive rather than of being supported, which might be effective in determining therapeutic outcome. However, the fact that revealing our shared situation was the unplanned result of the therapist's own needs cannot be ignored. In situations in which both the therapist and client share the same threat of war and terror, therapists should be aware of how their own exposure might interfere with the client's therapy.

There are situations during a therapeutic process in which the therapist is wise to share personal information with the family. This self-disclosure, when the therapist has control over the content and process of the disclosure, is intentionally offered for therapeutic purposes. In the illustration described above, however, the therapist had not controlled her disclosure to the client; rather, her response had been reactive to the mutual danger, to which client and therapist alike were exposed.

Terror as a Therapeutic Context

Therapy in Israel takes place under very stressful conditions that include, among other things, the ongoing terror as a dominant factor that affects the degree of closeness and/or distancing between therapist and family. As the therapist comes closer to the experience of terror, which is evoked by family members' evolving narratives about an event involving terror, she risks moving toward the pole of demonizing the other (in this case, those labeled as terrorists). In contrast, in distancing from family members' experience of terror, or in the absence of that experience of terror, the therapist can more readily shift the narratives and feelings in the session toward the humanization pole.

The overall political context of Israel in which therapeutic relationships are embedded depends largely on the current intensity and frequency of terrorist attacks. During periods of intense attacks, the probability is high that the attacks and related issues that families raise will also affect the therapist, while during periods of quiet, the issue, with little salience for both family and therapist, may hardly be raised at all. Additionally, the political context in Israel and the one experienced by Palestinian people are very dynamic and fluctuate between optimism and pessimism, as well as between humanization and dehumanization. The impact of these elements on the therapist and the family's interaction during therapy is very prominent.

The Therapist's Future Orientation

The therapist's personal level of optimism and hope for conflict resolution affect how she becomes involved with the family and her reaction to clinical material regarding terror and war that families bring to therapy. The therapist's level of involvement with the family as well as her reaction to the material regarding terror and war the family brings to treatment can shift her experiences between hope and despair. How much she shifts and in which direction depends in part on her personal, family of origin, and professional experiences of trauma and loss, both past (as with first or second-generation Holocaust survivors) and present (as with direct or indirect experience with families struggling with bereavement or PTSD as a result of terror). These variables are highly influential under less stressful conditions, let alone when therapists are coping with continuous stress.

Therapists' Coping Strategies

The ongoing effects of Israel's political and violence situation on therapists require them to develop special coping strategies that allow them to function well on both personal and professional levels. Living under continuous stress increases the need among therapists to care for themselves so as to remain efficient facilitators of healing and to minimize burnout. Therapists can employ a variety of self-care strategies, including those of physical, spiritual, and emotional care, as well as mutual support. Specific coping strategies relevant to our topic include, among others, minimizing the level of threat, balancing between demonization and humanization of the "other," shifting between identification with and disengagement from the experiences of client families, and empathizing with clients.

Reducing the Experienced Level of Threat in Order to Deal with the Horror of the Event

As a result of the ongoing nature of terror attacks, many therapeutic sessions take place shortly after the reports of a terror attack. Such announcements affect the entire population, even those who are, at most, indirectly harmed. People's reaction to terror events and news reports about them can be regarded as acute traumatic responses (Shalev et al. 2003).

Clients often hear the news of an attack first and then break it to their therapists. Using an internal process of minimization as a coping strategy can help the therapist focus on the therapeutic process rather than shifting away from her clients' feelings about the terror attack even when she experiences as high a level of threat as do the clients. It is important to emphasize that one must apply caution when using this strategy. The therapist needs to be careful to use this strategy optimally in order to maintain her professional competency. Optimal use of this coping mechanism calls for the therapist to take good care of herself as well both in and out of sessions.

In a supervision group session, "Ron" asked to discuss a family with whom he was working. The entire group and I (MS) knew that 4 days prior to the supervision session, Ron had intervened with a family who had lost one of their members in a terrorist attack, but Ron did not mention it. The group's and my reflections followed. When asked about his decision not to raise the attack, he offered detailed information, as if we were part of the media rather than a supervision group. I then asked why he had not chosen to bring such a horrible experience to the group and why he had shown no emotion in his narrative. In response, Ron, along with others in the group, said that they were so used to these terror attacks that they related to this one as just another attack among many rather than as a special event. Upon continuing to explore this attitude, I (MS) came to understand that minimization was the group's preferred way to cope with the situation. They were afraid that talking about their painful experiences might decrease their ability to cope with a chronic situation on a personal as well as at a professional level.

Between Demonization and Humanization of "The Enemy Other"

The following anecdote illustrates this strategy, in which humor was used in a group supervision session to address this axis:

> In response to another participant's comments about her fear of a possible terrorist penetration into her house, which was located in a village close to the Israeli-Lebanese border, "Eve" told the following story: Once we were talking about possible terrorist penetration into our village. The issue raised our anxiety until my neighbor, who has a wonderful sense of humor, said that of such a thing happened, she would use the "Jewish Mother Tactic." She said that because a terrorist is just a regular human being, when he got to her house he might be tired, hungry, and tense after walking all the way from Lebanon, crossing the border, and trying to hide from the soldiers. So, she said, first she would offer him some food and drink and in the meantime, she would find out what to do with him.... Thus, terrorists who were first perceived in a demonic light turned into regular human beings who needed care just like all of us.

Shifting Between Identification and Disengagement

This coping strategy can be used when working with clients who have been directly or indirectly involved in terrorist attacks. Identification, as we define it, refers to the over-involvement with the clients' experience and feelings of the therapist, who thereby becomes absorbed in it to the point that she may lose her professional judgment. Disengagement, on the other hand, involves the therapist's distancing herself from the client's experience in order to protect herself from becoming too absorbed. Moving between these two poles is often the therapist's way to search for the optimal degree of distance for any particular intervention. The following vignette illustrates the therapist's simultaneous identification with the client's pain to the point of crying, and her moving toward an emotional and cognitive disengagement from the pain and then finding the optimal distance in the interest of keeping her professional judgment and perspective.

> In a therapy session, a woman whose husband had been tragically killed by Arab gunmen tells of her notification of his death and her response to it. She had dialed his cellular phone right after talking to him, but this time she got no response. She started crying as she

> described the tension and horror she had experienced while unsuccessfully trying to call the police, family members, and friends. A few hours later, she fainted on being notified that he had in fact been murdered. Listening to her story, I (RM) started shivering and tears filled my eyes. Thinking to myself, I realized that I felt sorry for her but also realized how vulnerable we all are.
> Recognizing the importance of being with her, I was able to stop my own chain of thoughts and return more fully to her. After a moment of silence, I said, "your world has been shattered, never to be the same again." In this sequence, disengagement was followed by empathy (Malkinson et al. 2005).

Empathizing

The therapist's ability to stay with her client's pain within the therapeutic process and, at the same time, to understand the pain and losses of the enemy "other" is a central skill in managing the effects of ongoing stress. There is a parallel process in which the therapist must be able to empathize with both the pain and the anger of the injured family and the losses and suffering of the "other." Empathizing with the enemy has the potential to reduce the therapist's own level of anxiety and anger, which helps her to contain the family's feelings. When the bereaved families themselves adopt this empathic stance toward the other, they find a source of hope. Two illustrations will be presented: empathy as first experienced by a therapist conducting a research study and second as experienced between bereaved Israeli and Palestinian families.

To illustrate this shift from disengagement to empathy, in this case, for the "other," we describe the research of a colleague (TL), who works with us at the university investigating the experiences and attitudes of both Israeli and Palestinian children. She told us:

> The intensity of the experience of the research interviews was so profound that although in daily life I try to be politically involved, I found that during the period of collecting data, I felt it was too much and I neutralized any political activity of mine. I felt a need to come "clean" of attitudes toward the various villages I visited for purposes of my study. This was a terrible shake-up: to move from one Palestinian village to another and see real and true suffering, especially that of children. It was a surreal [situation] to be 1 day in Bethlehem with a colleague from Bait Jalap [an Arab town] and a month later to visit Gilo [a Jewish suburb of Jerusalem].

Children's Visions of the Conflict

So far, we have focused on how therapists and researchers, ourselves included, experience the ramifications of the ongoing conflict in the Middle East, both as individuals and as professionals. Now, we add the experiences of children. The children of today are the adults of tomorrow. How do they envision the conflict? What are their attitudes regarding how and when the conflict will end and the safety and coherence of their life restored?

Lavi and Solomon's (2005) and Solomon and Laufer's (2005) studies of 552 Palestinian and 741Israeli children's view of the conflict revealed similar patterns for Israeli (age range 12–16) and Palestinian children, (ages 10–14). Children were asked about their attitudes toward resuming peace talks between the Israelis and the Palestinians. Of the Palestinian children, 41 % reported thinking that the talks should not resume at all, as did 39 % of their Israeli peers. Fifty-one percent of the Palestinian children wanted to resume talks in comparison to 36 % of the Israeli children. Finally, 8 % of the Palestinian children and 25 % of the Israeli children wanted to hold off on resuming talks. Apparently, the perception of "Me" and of the "Other" is a two-way mirror.

According to the researchers (Tamar Lavi, personal communication, June, 2004) the children's responses regarding the end of the conflict represented three distinct voices, as follows:

The Aggressive View

From the aggressive standpoint, the "other" is viewed as the bad party who is responsible for the evil and who therefore deserves revenge. One Israeli child (a boy, age 13) said, "We will bombard the Arabs, we will expel the Arabs; in the end we will kill them all." A Palestinian (a boy, age 14) shared this aggressive stance, reporting, "Last night I dreamed that my friends blew up five houses and killed soldiers…. Only then a victory was achieved, the victory that everyone wished for." These children expressed this aggressive view in a negative activist manner, advocating the expulsion or killing of the "other" as a solution to one's distress. This is a black or white attitude with minimal ability to empathize with the "other."

The Pessimistic View

Disbelief and feelings of helplessness and despair characterize this stance. One Israeli girl, age 12, answered that "The killing will continue and will never end." (Unfortunately we don't have access to a quote of a pessimistic view expressed by a Palestinian child). One possible outcome of continuous conflict is the feeling of exhaustion expressed in a passive, negative attitude toward any solution. Such pessimism provides one with a way of disengaging oneself from a situation perceived as unresolved and distressing.

The Optimistic View

Optimistic views can take many forms, which represent many voices of hope and resolution. One 11-year-old Israeli boy premised his optimism about the future of Israel on his religious beliefs, opining, "When the Messiah comes, everything will be all right." A Palestinian girl, age 13, expressed her optimistic view as follows: "Last night I dreamt that an earthquake hit the settlement like they hit Armenia. Only then the Israelis turned towards us and asked to make peace. I woke up with tears in my eyes."

Optimistic views are expressed in various ways among the children, both Israelis and Palestinians, regarding hopes for conflict resolution. In one optimistic view, extinguishing the other is the preferred outcome. In a different variation of the optimistic view, negotiation is the way to end the conflict between the sides. Quotations from both sides suggest that living under continuous stress affects children's levels of awareness of death, foreshortens their sense of future, inclines children toward holding a generally pessimistic future orientation, and increases their vulnerability to the consequences of PTSD and of complicated grief (Pynoos and Nader 1990).

When Subject and the "Enemy Other" Are in the Same Boat of Grief and Pain

We conclude by elaborating on a narrative that increases our own level of optimism and hope and which also facilitates a greater national awareness of each other on both sides and consequently results in a mutual dialogue. One of us (RM) is involved with a project, the Bereaved Parents' Forum for Peace (www.theparentscircle.com). This group of bereaved Israeli and Palestinian families, all of whom have lost dear ones to the Israeli-Palestinian conflict, are constructing a narrative in which the pain of grief can become a resource for promoting peace. The Bereaved Parents' Forum for Peace beautifully illustrates the process of empathizing with the "other," which we have described above as a coping strategy for therapists' working with people bereaved by war and terror.

The Forum began as a group of bereaved Israeli families in November of 1995, following the assassination of Prime Minister Yitzhak Rabin. Later, bereaved Palestinian parent members of the Parent Forum for Peace quoted the assassinated Egyptian President Sadat, who, upon his visit to Israel in 1977, said, "Peace is the only way to stop the bloodshed." In the context of war and political conflict, this group has constructed a narrative that demonstrates that the meanings of the loss of a child can take many forms.

The long-term goals of The Parents Circle, or the Bereaved Parents Forum for Peace, as stated by the Forum's members in the founding meeting, are as follows:

Our Long Term Goals—Promoting Reconciliation

The long-term goals of the Families Forum are to promote reconciliation between the Israeli and Palestinian societies. The Families Forum aims to play a crucial role spearheading a reconciliation process between Israelis and Palestinians. Such a process will allow both sides to come to terms with past suffering. The reconciliation process will provide a firm basis for the difficult measures a future agreement will include by recognizing responsibility of both sides for the past.

By allowing both Israelis and Palestinians to come to terms with the consequences of the escalating violence, both sides will begin to change their beliefs, which are at the root of the conflict. Currently, the parties are too immersed in their own pain to be willing to acknowledge the other's suffering. By acknowledging the personal narratives of victims of both sides, a new chapter in the relations between the sides may, at last, begin. Past activities of the Families Forum have generated empathy for bereaved families of the opposing side by gradually exposing both societies to each other's loss.

Palestinians and Israelis have so far avoided recognizing the pain of the other side. A reconciliation process initiated by the Families Forum can put victims who refuse to revenge their loss and choose to reconcile at the forefront of public awareness. In doing so, they will humanize both sides and will act as an example to the Israeli and Palestinian people.

A few observations can be made, based on the Forum's statement. First, the Forum shows us that a voluntary organization can establish inter-group contact with the aim of establishing a purposeful "living next to each other" and living with the "other as enemy," which in turn moves families toward the humanization end of the Humanization-Demonization axis.

Second, the Forum for Peace exemplifies how individual loss, which takes place in a national context, can be extended into constructing a meta-value in which the self or the "me" and the "other-enemy" are in the same boat. This is a unique way to construct a healing meaning out of loss,

Third, the Forum of Bereaved Families for Peace illustrates the potential for a self-help organization's empowerment without either professional or political involvement. The following quotes illustrate how the parent members of the Family Forum for Peace verbalize their thoughts and feelings.

> Peace is the only way to end the bloodshed.
> The pain [of parents on both sides] is the same; grief is the same.
> Grief can give us the strength to do everything, to bring peace.
> Pain and grief know no boundaries.

Where pain and hope co-exist there is no better way to conclude our paper than with these words:

> For everything there is a season and a time for every matter under heaven:
> a time to plant and a time to pluck up what is planted;
> a time to be born, and a time to die;
> a time to kill and a time to heal;
> a time to break down and a time to build up;
> a time to weep and a time to laugh;
> a time to mourn and a time to dance;
> a time to cast away stones, and a time to gather stones together;
> a time to embrace, and a time to refrain from embracing;
> a time to seek, and a time to lose;
> a time to keep, and a time to cast away;

a time to rend, and a time to sew;
a time to keep silence and a time to speak;
a time to love and a time to hate;
a time for war and a time for peace.
(Ecclesiastes 3, 1–9)

References

Bliech, A., Gelkopf, M., & Solomon, Z. (2003). Exposure to terrorism, stress-related mental health symptoms, and coping behaviors among a nationally representative sample in Israel. *Journal of the American Medical Association, 290*, 612–620.

Klein, M. (1975). *Envy and gratitude and other works 1946–1963*. London, UK: The Hogarth Press.

Lavi, T., & Solomon, Z. (2005). Palestinian youth of the Intifada: PTSD and future orientation. *Journal of the American Academy of Child and Adolescent Psychiatry, 44*(11), 1183–1176.

Malkinson, R., Rubin, S., & Witztum, E. (2005). Terror, trauma and bereavement: Implications for theory and therapy. In Y. Danieli, D. Brom, & J. Sills (Eds.). *The Trauma of terrorism: Sharing knowledge and shared care. An international handbook* (pp. 467–481). New York, NY: Haworth.

Pynoos, R. S., & Nader, K. (1990). Children's exposure to violence and traumatic death. *Annals of Psychiatry, 20*, 334–344.

Scharff, D., & Scharff, J. (1987). *Object relations family therapy*. New York, NY: Jason Aronson.

Shalev, A.Y., Adessky, R., Boker, R., Bargau, N., Cooper, R., & Freedman, S. (2003). *Clinical interventions for survivors of prolonged adversities*. In R. Ursano, C. S. Fullerton, & A. E. Norwood (Eds.), Terrorism and disaster (pp. 162–188). New York, NY: Cambridge University Press.

Solomon, Z., & Laufer, A. (2005). In the shadow of terror: Changes in world assumptions in Israeli youth. In Y. Daniel, D., Brom, & J. Sills (Eds.). *The trauma of terrorism: Sharing knowledge and shared care. An international handbook* (pp. 353–364). New York, NY: Haworth.

References

Reflections on Growing Up in a War Zone: Understanding War and Building Peace

Sanja Rolovic and Roxana Llerena-Quinn

Introduction

In the aftermath of 9/11, in 2002, the American Family Therapy Academy (AFTA) endorsed a new interest group to invite dialogue about war, its effects on our lives and on the lives of our children. Re-awakened from complacency by recent events in the United States, when terror descended from the skies, our eyes turned to the world, to its war zones and communities in conflict. We noticed anew the reality of war and the elusiveness of peace. One of us (SR), who is personally connected to the reality of wars in the former Yugoslavia, initiated the interest group as an opportunity to work on peace with colleagues of AFTA. Initially, our goal was to develop a curriculum anchored in systemic understandings for teaching peace practices to our children and to our communities.

Although much has been written about the effects of trauma and violence on children and adults (Apfel and Simon 1996; Garbarino and Kostelny 1996; Herman 1992; Terr 1990) and many useful manuals have been developed (Kliman 2005), less has been written about the processes that generate war or promote peace (Botcharova 2001; Kliman and Llerena-Quinn 2002; Weingarten 2003). Surprisingly, little information of this nature can be found in the professional literature, especially in the narrative and family systems arena. What knowledge does exist is neither well known nor systematically used in the mental health field.

The dangers of war and need for peace have been amply documented. In the twentieth century alone, 115 million lives, 63 million of whom were civilians, were lost to war. As more enemies are constructed, the need for peace education becomes

Editors' note: First published in 2005, American Family Therapy Academy Monograph Series.

S. Rolovic (✉)
New York, NY, USA
e-mail: jrolovic@verizon.net

R. Llerena-Quinn
Department of Outpatient Psychiatry, Boston Children's Hospital,
Harvard Medical School, Boston, MA, USA

T. Nelson, H. Winawer (eds.), *Critical Topics in Family Therapy*,
AFTA SpringerBriefs in Family Therapy, DOI 10.1007/978-3-319-03248-1_3,

more evident than ever. Although many people around the world care deeply about building peace, our maps of war and peace are drawn in relation to our respective locations and experiences, which bear the traces of our collective and relational histories. Thus, the field needs to develop an interpretive framework that will allow us to probe more deeply into these experiences in hopes of uncovering those processes that contribute to creating and targeting the *other*, and those that create and promote peace (Ceadel 1989; Schwalbe et al. 2000). For the purposes of this article, peace is defined as more than the absence of war or personal violence, as it also involves the absence of inequality, discrimination, or structural violence (Toffler and Toffler 1995).

The Beginning: AFTA 2003

With these ideas in mind, AFTA's "Growing Up in the War Zone" interest group met for the first time in 2003. The interest group committed itself to continued learning about the processes that generate "war narratives" (those that promote violence and retaliation) and "peace narratives" (those that generate empowerment, inclusion, forgiveness, and reconciliation), and those that generate dialogues between *us* and the other. Our hope is to construct a common language that can be applied to various contexts and settings, drawing from the experiences of people from diverse personal, national, and international social contexts, whose experiences, work, or interests connect them in some way to the "war zone."

We began our first interest group discussion with several colleagues in the room by introducing ourselves and reflecting on our respective direct and indirect experiences with war and violence. In 2003, September 11th was still at the forefront of the conversation in this country. This initial session helped us to define what we mean by "the war zone" and to delineate the multiple ways in which we are connected to the experience of war and peace.

Defining the War Zone

In 5,600 years of written history, 14,600 wars have been recorded, that is, 2–3 wars for each year of human history (Hillman 2004). Does this consistency prove that war is or might be "normal"? Although this possibility shocks our morality and wounds our idealism, we need to acknowledge the ubiquity of war and be humbled by the unimaginable tragedy that we humans can bring on one another. At the same time, we are reminded that compassion, as much as cruelty, is another aspect of our humanness and both can be life changing. War is a life-changing event that exceeds the demands of everyday reality.

War zones include areas of frank warfare (overt or covert) between nations or between factions within nations. War zones can be sites of war or of other kinds of communal violence. "War participants" are those people directly affected as victims or survivors, soldiers, bystanders, witnesses, and members of the communities at war.

We define living in the "war zone" broadly, so as to include different voices. Of course, we also recognize fundamental differences among the experiences of these participants. Fear and terminal thinking, that is, the expectation that one will be killed and that one certainly will not live to old age, are commonly reported themes in war zones, particularly for children with first-hand experience of severe personal loss. Thirty-five percent of sixth to twelfth graders living in urban, inner-city areas in the United States also report similar beliefs (Garbarino et al. 1991 as cited in Garbarino and Kostelny 1996).

Child development, the process of becoming fully human, can be profoundly altered for children growing up in the war zone. Unsafe environments challenge the development of children's trust, autonomy, initiative, and sense of agency. The child's map of the world is profoundly altered in all its cognitive and affective capacities (Garbarino and Kostelny 1996). The social roles available to all of us (as parent, sister, brother, friend, student, etc.) are also threatened while new ones appear, including refugee, soldier, terrorist, and target (Garbarino and Kostelny 1996).

Children grow up in war zones around the world: the former Yugoslavia, a country destroyed by ethnic war, Iraq, Israel, Palestine, Rwanda, Colombia, and many other places. War zones include those communities in which every child has witnessed or expects to witness violence and has been or expects to be violated (Apfel and Simon 1996).

Mapping the War Zone: The Impact of Location and Experience

Our maps of war and peace are profoundly affected by location and experience. At our first meeting in 2003, participants discussed the multiple ways in which they felt connected to growing up in a war zone. Their connections were distinct and personal, varying in relation to geographical distance, how long it had been since their war experience, the level of war's impact on their lives, and the level of personal safety they and their loved ones had experienced. Their connections varied as well with their communities' historical location in a given conflict.

Two participants had direct experience with current or recent conflict areas outside the United States. One had worked with "leftist students" in war-torn areas of Colombia until it became "too risky" to keep going back. Another (SR) came from the former Yugoslavia. Still others reported connections to war zones through family members who had been persecuted during the pogroms (systematic violence against Jews in the ghettos of Eastern Europe) and the Holocaust or whose relatives had been prisoners of war during World War II. The group represented people from different historical locations of conflict, including both members of communities seen as targets or as perpetrators. Some participants came to learn. One found the topic relevant to her work in the area of loss, which is an inevitable consequence of war.

All present had been affected by the events of September 11. Like most history-shattering events, this catastrophe's extremity and immediacy served as a template for thinking about other tragic events. The awareness that the long-lasting impact of this atrocity will go beyond the personal and will be linked to a larger history made us realize that it is essential to learn from those who had to live out and struggle with some of the defining issues that follow.

With these quandaries in mind, we watched a videotape of a Bosnian woman named Ana, whom one of us (SR) had interviewed in her office. The tape illustrated a session with the "other"; the therapist is a member of a community that is perceived as the perpetrator group while the client is a member of a community that is perceived as the victim group. When, as people and as professionals, we are faced with events that surpass our limits of experience or training, when the relationship of private experience and memory is dependent to a broader understanding of history, our roles and identities, as we know them, are challenged. When, as a result of war and war-like atrocities, the demands of a reality exceed our expectations, politics becomes inseparable from psyche. Aria and SR, a patient and a therapist, met each other face-to-face, with the brutality of war and disasters present in the "therapeutic space" between them.

At such times, the relationship between the "me" and the "other" transcends personal experience and we are reminded of the vulnerability and multidimensionality of our identities. In order to arrive at a place that enhances healing and forgiveness, it was first necessary to acknowledge the power of the deeply ingrained images and emotions tied to all those (the Serbs in this case) responsible for the destruction of lives close to Aria. The cultural imperative to hate the aggressor parallels and fortifies loyalty to the victims of the aggressor group and to the larger culture, in Ana's case, Bosnian culture (Hoffman 2004).

In addition, the need to link the personal experience to a "larger" collective experience ("what is done to my people") in times of atrocities seems to be not only a moral imperative, but also a prerequisite for self-preservation. It is likely that, while those processes work toward restoring the sense of self, the self and the other both experience losses and gains (Volkan et al. 2002).

The videotape presentation brought into focus the need to find new ways to think about self and the other that do not require us to *annihilate the other* order to *preserve the self.* The need for an expanded perspective on the self and the other seemed appropriate, and so we start the exploration with ourselves.

The Continuum of War: Two Perspectives on Expanding the Self

Sanja's Story The war in the former Yugoslavia, my homeland, had become a turning point in my own life and work. Throughout the past 10 years since the war began, I had come to realize that my professional (and personal) identity was being challenged in significant ways. I was compelled to reexamine my cultural heritage and to question the identity I had grown up with and the one I felt had been politically imposed on me. In 1995, I began working with refugees from the former Yugoslavia, including those seeking political asylum. In order to do this work, I had to raise my awareness about the dangers and temptations of seeing the world through ethnocentric lenses, which foster *not seeing the other* and isolation.

I came to the US in 1988 to study family therapy. I came from Yugoslavia, a country that, at the time, many people would mistake for any other neighboring country, like Rumania, or Poland, or the Czech Republic (then Czechoslovakia). I had grown up and lived in Belgrade, the capital city of Yugoslavia, whose cosmopolitanism and globally oriented attitudes had been the county's pride.

The war in "my country," now "the Former Yugoslavia," began in 1991. That same year, Yugoslavia, as I knew it, exploded. I stopped being a Yugoslav and became a "Serb" In the years to come, many died in one of the bloodiest and most immoral ethnic wars of the late twentieth century. The pressures of nationalism and the aggression of war had changed the face of my homeland. Mix in some historical facts, spiced by national myths, and we were transformed into "is" and "them." The cosmopolitan, coexisting ethnic mix of Serbs, Croats, Bosnian Muslims, and Kosovars who had lived in peace and unity for 50 years was demolished and the process of dehumanizing our neighbors began. For the past 10 years, I have heard stories about the consequences from the peoples of Bosnia, Croatia, Serbia, and Kosovo. I have worked with the "all"—Muslims, Orthodox Christians, and Catholics.

I have worked with the "other" and I am the "other." I am a "former Yugoslav," a psychologist with a degree from the former Yugoslavia. I am now a Serb, living in New York City and, because all former Yugoslavs share the same language, I have become a "trauma specialist" for my former compatriots of every ethnicity. In the past 10 years, I lived through the amazing experience of watching my country becoming alive—in a negative way—in front of the eyes of the world. My experience of "my country" has been taken away from me. Working with refugees and all those displaced by the atrocities of war has taught me important lessons. What can we learn from 10 years of the wars in "the Balkans"? The following clinical vignette of a young Bosnian woman provides some answers.

Encountering Hatred: "If You Gave Me a Serbian Baby, I Could Kill It"

Ana (as I will call her) came to see me (SR) on several occasions. She described how, by the end of the war in Bosnia and after the massacre in Srebrenica, she had come to hate. Although nothing had happened directly to her family and she had been able to make a decent living, hearing about mass rapes and killings and the fact that "nobody was doing anything" made her sick.

After immigrating to the US, she found a job, went to college, and tried to put the past behind her. However, she felt a huge pain inside, a heavy load that she said got in the way of love. The first time this young woman encountered a Serbian, this "other" was at a theater group she had joined. Although she initially wanted to leave, she stayed and discovered that this person did not have a clue what had been done in her name. Being able to tell this person the truth and being believed made a difference. "I did not know you and yet, I hated you. It was your people who did the harm," she had told this woman (the "other"). "Now I feel different."

What had helped Ana to put down her hatred? Telling her story of what had happened (setting the record straight), being believed, knowing that "they" (the Serbs or at least some of them) had not known what was being done in their name—all these experiences helped.

Did my listening to and believing Ana's story and her account of history (in which, after all, I was "the other") validate the reality of her experience of the brutalities done to her people by "my" people?

In the therapy room, we—this young woman who grew up in Bosnia and I, who grew up in Serbia—shared her war story. In the room, looking at each other, we were together, two women, each of us a victim and a survivor of our forever-changed worlds. I would like to think my recognition of her tragedy brought her some relief. I know that bearing witness brought me some reprieve from the heavy burden of "national" responsibility I have been carrying. It may be that accepting the national responsibility while bearing witness liberated us both.

Roxana's Story: Witnessing From a Privileged Safety

I grew up in Peru, a country with large disparities in the distribution of land, wealth, and power. Peru is a place whose original inhabitants have the least power and wealth. The country was built on the shoulders of a colonized indigenous population and, for a while, with the help of African slaves. Disparities persist today despite the agrarian land reform in the late 60s and 70s, which preceded a bloody internal conflict that began in 1980 and lasted for over a decade into the 1990s. By the time the Shining Path's leader was captured, 30,000 lives, mostly innocent, had been lost on all sides.

Because of my immigration, I have watched the armed conflicts in Peru and elsewhere from afar, from the United States and from the safety of my home. In the United States, I have worked in urban communities where our youth are dying, but invariably at night, I return home where the shots cannot be heard. One click and the war goes on, one click and the news goes off. Disturbing images stay with me for a while, but then I fall asleep in a warm bed, not hungry, not afraid of bombs or stray bullet hitting my home or my children.

Still, I have strong visceral reactions to what the news shows me, knowing the news reports only partial stories, sanitized versions of the truth. Anyone out there could be me—or my family—in either camp. Nothing I have done has earned me the privilege of not being there. I imagine myself there, being there with my children. I want to stop imagining. Moving closer to home, I think of the mothers I work with who come from parts of the city where children dodge bullets now. As disturbing as this feels, it is the closest I get to the horror.

I speak from a place of privileged safety; I cannot fully appreciate the horror, the costs, or the resilience of those who live at the center of war, terror, or violence. I speak of peace from *that* place. What does this privilege help me to see? What does it prevent me from seeing? How do the very safe and the very unsafe make decisions on war? In 1992, I received a phone call from Peru. It was from a Peruvian grassroots worker, whom I had met a year earlier while she was in Boston. Amanda, as I will call her, was crying and pleading for the lives of her children. Her son had been beaten and the family threatened with death; she needed to leave the country. A year earlier, another grassroots worker, Maria Moyano, in similar circumstances, had been shot in front of her children. Something in Amanda's voice signaled the gravity of the situation.

Paralyzed by fear, I thought of her children being killed because I did not know how to help her. How do you respond to a request like this one? Who threatened you? I asked. Was it the Army or the Shining Path? Subconsciously, I wanted to peg her into a category. What kind of "other" is she? What side is she on? She would not say, which made it difficult to get help from the official institutions. With help from someone I knew very well in the church, Amanda and her family went underground overnight and, much later, were granted asylum in Sweden. I did not hear from her until almost 2 years after, when she came to visit me in the United States. I asked her then if she had been a member of Shining Path. She said, "No," almost amused by my need to label her. She said she had no political affiliations; her only politics were the politics of hunger and the starvation of the children in her community. She was a leader and organizer, which made her visible and suspect to people on all sides of the conflict. The conflict had pitted villagers against villagers.

Far from the home where we were both born, Amanda told me her story. Born in the same land, but in very different contexts, our lives unfolded geographically near, yet worlds apart. How does one become the "other"? How do privilege, poverty, and injustice stand in the way of peace? Amanda, one of the many invisible people of my childhood, came a long way to my place of safety with a gift. Her story allowed me to learn more about myself and about what needs to be done to build peace. I can see her now through her own eyes with the perspective her eyes have lent to mine. Without such understanding, "one is really alone in the other's presence" (Lugones 1990) and our world is much smaller and much less safe.

AFTA 2004: Inviting More Voices

In the summer of 2004, the second meeting of our "Growing Up in a War Zone" interest group at AFTA took place in San Francisco. An overwhelming number of colleagues came to the interest group, in contrast to the few who attended the first meeting. We explored the relationship between "me and the other," from the smallest cell of conflict to conflictual relations between nations and groups of people.

Our colleagues from Israel, Yael Geron, Ruth Malkinson (in absentia), and Michal Shamai, delivered their message in English, their second language, amidst concerns from the audience about the sound quality of the presentation. In this context of differential language privilege, *the English-speaking us"*—the American audience—listened to the *foreign-speaking "other"*—the Israeli presenters—as they described their work with those who are differently "other" to them. The setting provided a poignant metaphor for all that might be required as we begin dialogues outside familiar borders.

Yael, Michal, and Ruth briefly introduced us to their work with families who had suffered trauma as a result of violent conflict, discussing the ways they deal in therapy with the issue of the "enemy," "the other." Their presentation focused on what happens when the therapist and the family share the same trauma and their efforts for peace. Kamya (2005) and Weingarten (2005) provided their reflections on the presentation, helping us make the transition to group discussion. This meeting prompted us (SR and RLQ) to continue to explore the processes involved in "othering." Below, we elaborate on some of the concepts and models we have found useful in expanding our discussion.

Reflections on the "Other"

What is it to be them, what is to be ourselves in their eyes? Can we travel to each other's worlds? What do we need to do to see people beyond their stereotypes? What are the socioeconomic/political structures that expose people to damage? What happens to me when I don't see the other? What are the consequences to "us" for the failure to see the "other" (Canales 2001)? These questions invite us to look at ourselves through the eyes of others and to look at the others as they see themselves in an effort to see each other more clearly. A more empathic understanding of each other may facilitate building narratives of peace instead of retaliation.

Weis (1995) defines othering as "that process which serves to mark and name those thought to be different from oneself' (p. 18). Charon (1992) suggests, "It is through others that we come to see and define self, and it is our ability to role-take that allows us to see ourselves through others" (p. 107). These two definitions highlight processes that mark the other as separate and different from the self but also as essential to defining who we are. Thus, the self and the other are constructed as a result of a relational process. Based on these assumptions, othering can be used as an *exclusionary* or as an *inclusionary* process. Both processes exist in a context of power and power relationships. The difference between inclusionary and exclusionary othering lies in how power is used and in their consequences (Canales 2001).

Exclusionary *othering* uses power within relationships for the purposes of domination and subordination. It is a process whereby a dominant group defines an inferior group into existence (Canales 2001). This process entails defining the self against the other rather than in relation to the other. Exclusionary othering is one of several processes that can be used to create and reproduce inequalities (Schwalbe et al. 2000). This process entails the invention of categories and of ideas about what marks people as belonging to these categories (Fine 1994).

Consequences for the "targets" of othering include alienation, marginalization, decreased opportunities, internalized oppression, and exclusion (Canales 2000; Charon 1992; Fine 1994; Madrid 1992). Such othering, or dehumanization of the other, has negative consequences for human development, self-esteem, health promotion, and healing. When we see the other without regard to context, we only have access to stereotyped representations that do harm and perpetuate the invisibility of the excluded "other." We can even justify killing the other, whom we have dehumanized (Kliman and Llerena-Quinn 2002). In contexts of extreme conflict, *othered* or dehumanized, individuals can even be willing to die in order to restore the loss self-respect (Canales 2000). When afraid, vulnerable, targeted, and exposed, the "biology of fear" takes over and tomorrow no longer exists. Shamed and devalued, we become dehumanized enough to kill (Kenneth Hardy, personal communication, June 23, 2004). Examples of this dynamic include suicide bombers and others who die along with their enemies, with restored sense of self or group respect in mind.

Othering can also be an inclusionary process. According to Canales (1998, 2001), *inclusionary othering* is a process aimed at utilizing power for transformation and coalition building. Inclusionary othering expands the boundaries for defining the self-in-relation to the other; difference is re-conceptualized as a tool for creativity, exploration, critique, and empowerment Power is used to create transformational relationships, in which the consequences are consciousness raising (new knowledge/information), a sense of community (connection), shared power (power with, rather than over, the other), and inclusion. Role-taking, the process of imagining the world from the perspective of another, is an important dynamic step for inclusionary othering. Role-taking can also be understood as empathy, informed empathy, or insight. As we imagine, so we act (Charon 1992).

When people take the role of the other, they attempt to view the world from the other's perspective and begin to understand the meaning of the other's world. Such understandings are central for connection and for empowerment to occur. When people are unable to see the different other as they see themselves, they rely on stereotypical representations of those they perceive as different, which further perpetuates the separation between self and other. When we are unable to see the world from the perspective of other individuals or groups, we fail to interact or truly connect. Whatever interaction exists without empathy is based on misconceptions or stereotypes (Canales 2001).

Expanding the Self to Include the Other

At our 2004 Meeting, Yael, Michal, and Ruth described their work with the enemy other. Their presentation provided an example of how to expand the self to include the other. Through their capacity to take on each other's roles as bereaved Israeli and Palestinian mothers and to see the world they share as mothers whose children, husbands, brothers are in harm's way, the speakers expanded their sense of self and shared with us images of a humanized other. In that space, "enemies" are transformed into allies—mothers bereaved by war—working together for peace.

In this article, we provided two examples of the process of expanding the self. Confronted with the realization that we cannot turn away from the realities of war, which has already changed the landscape of our daily lives, and go back to the familiar, we each asked ourselves, "What have I learned about myself from the "other"?"

The "therapeutic" work with the young Bosnian woman in the videotape first involved stopping the cycle of hate by listening and understanding her world. Ana realized that her hate had blinded her to the point of wishing to avenge by killing a Serbian baby. The process first required the powerful outsider (SR) to acknowledge the affective, moral, and political responsibility for the damage to Ana's life and to the lives of those around liar. Then (and only then), after differences in power and responsibility had been acknowledged and accounted for, the dyad was transformed into allies who share the common ground of mutual loss and suffering. Through SR's entering Ana's world, both therapist and client learned something about both of their worlds. This process possibly lends some hope to "peace building practices."

In the second story, between a Peruvian and a Peruvian American, RLQ acknowledged that distance from the event in a place of privileged safety versus direct exposure (and all that is in between) is one of the determining factors that influences our ability to walk in the shoes of the other. Born in the same land, but in very different contexts, the lives of these two women unfolded geographically near, yet worlds apart.

Amanda's story allowed RLQ to learn more about ways in which privilege, poverty, and injustice stand in the way of peace. It allowed her to realize that one's "place of safety" is much smaller and much less safe when "exclusionary" processes take over. Moreover, expanding the self by including the world of the other requires a commitment to self-awareness and to a continuous examination of the socioeconomic/political structures that expose people to damage. It requires a commitment to avoid producing structures that harm and to work toward repairing both the intended and non-intended consequences of these structures (Canales 2001; Charon 1992; Hardy and Laszloffy 2002; Kamya and Trimble 2002; Kliman and Llerena-Quinn 2002)

Conclusion

The goal of the AFTA interest group, "Growing Up in a War Zone," is to understand war narratives and to learn to build peace narratives. This article provided a summary and some reflections on the ideas that have been exchanged in the group to this date. Our group acknowledged the ubiquity of war. We were reminded that compassion, as much as cruelty, is an important aspect of our human-ness. The fact that both can be life changing makes the need to work on peace more urgent than ever. As we explore processes that lead to peace, we noted the importance of situating ourselves, naming the places where we speak from and their relation to the war zones. We found this to be important because each of our respective maps of war and peace is profoundly affected by our social location and experience. The maps can help us distinguish the territories where we are guests and need guidance from the territories where others need our guidance. Defining the war zone broadly allowed us to include many voices in our beginning exploration of the processes that lead to conflict and those that lead to peace. As a result, voices from different parts of the world have been reaching us, bringing their unique messages and hopes with them.

References

Apfel, R., & Simon, B. (1996). Introduction. In R. Apfel & B. Simon (Eds.), *Minefields in their hearts: The mental health of children in war and communal violence* (pp. 1–17). New Haven, CT: Yale University Press.

Botcharova, O. (2001). Implementation of track two diplomacy: Developing a model of forgiveness. In R. G. Helmick & R. L. Petersen (Eds.), *Forgiveness and reconciliation: Religion, public policy, & conflict transformation* (pp. 269–294). Philadelphia, PA: Templeton Foundation Press.

Canales, M. K. (1998). *Changing perceptions of the other: Teaching practices of doctorally prepared Latina faculty*. Unpublished doctoral dissertation, University of Wisconsin Madison.

Canales, M. K. (2001). Othering: Towards an understanding of difference. *Advanced Nursing Science*, *22*, 16–31.

Ceadel, M. (1989). *Thinking about peace and war*. Oxford: Oxford University Press. Available at http://www.ppu.org.uk/learn/peaceed/pe_debate.html

Charon, J. M. (1992). *Symbolic interactionism: An introduction, an interpretation, an integration* (4th ed.). Englewood Cliffs, NJ: Prentice Hall.

Fine, M. (1994). Working the hyphens: Reinventing self and other in qualitative research. In N. K. Denzin & Y. S. Lincoln (Eds.), *Handbook of qualitative research* (pp. 70–82). Thousand Oaks, CA: Sage Publications.

Garbarino, J., & Kostelny, K. (1996). What do we need to know to understand children in war and community violence. In R. Apfel & B. Simon (Eds.), *Minefields in their hearts: The mental health of children in war and communal violence* (pp. 33–51). New Haven, CT: Yale University Press.

Hardy, K. V., & Laszloffy, T. A. (2002). Couple therapy using a multicultural perspective. In A. S. Gurman & N. S. Jacobson (Eds.), *Clinical handbook of couple therapy* (3rd ed., pp. 569–593). New York, NY: Guilford.

Herman, J. L. (1992). *Trauma and recovery*. New York, NY: Basic Books.

Hillman, J. (2004). *A terrible love of war*. New York, NY: Penguin.

Hoffman, E. (2004). *After such knowledge*. New York, NY: Public Affairs.

Kamya, H. & Trimble, D. (2002). Response to injury: Toward ethical construction of the other. *Journal of Systemic Therapies*, *21*, 19–29.

Kamya, H. (2005). The Impact of war on children and families: Their stories, my Own Stories. In J. Kliman (Ed.).In J. Kliman (Ed.), *Introduction to the AFTA Monograph Series. Touched by war zones, near and far: Oscillations of despair and hope* (pp. 29-32). Washington, DC: American Family Therapy Academy.

Kliman, J. (2005). *My book about war: A guided activity work-book for children, families, and teachers to promote healthy expression, learning, and coping*. Available at http://www.childrenspsychologicalhealthcenter.org/content/view/25/44/

Kliman, J., & Llerena-Quinn, R. (2002). Dehumanizing and rehumanizing responses to September 11. *Journal of Systemic Therapies*, *21*, 8–18.

Lugones, M. (1990). Playfulness, "world" traveling and loving perception. In G. Anzaldua (Ed.), *Making face, making soul: Haciendo caras* (pp. 390–402). San Francisco, CA: Aunt Lute Foundation Books.

Madrid, A. (1992). Missing people and others: Joining together to expand the circle. In M. L. Anderson & P. H. Collins (Eds.), *Race, class and gender: An anthology* (pp. 6–11). Belmont, CA: Wadsworth.

Schwalbe, M., Godwin, S., Holde, D., Schrock, D., & Thompson, S. (2000). Generic processes in the reproduction of inequality: An interactionist analysis. *Social Forces*, *70*, 419–452.

Terr, L. (1990). *Too scared to cry*. New York, NY: Harper & Row.

Toffler, A., & Toffler, H. (1995). *War and antiwar: Survival at the dawn of the 21st century*. Boston, MA: Little, Brown & Company.

Volkan, V. D., Ast, G., & Greer, W. F., Jr. (Eds.). (2002). *The third Reich in the unconscious*. New York, NY: Brunner-Routledge.

Weingarten, K. (2003). *Common shock*. New York, NY: New American Library.

Weingarten, K. (2005). Reflections on families in the war zone: narratives of "Me" and the "Other" in the course of therapy. In J. Kliman (Ed.), *Introduction to the AFTA Monograph Series. Touched by war zones, near and far: Oscillations of despair and hope* (pp. 26-28). Washington, DC: American Family Therapy Academy.

Weis, L. (1995). Identity formation and the processes of "othering": Unraveling sexual threads. *Educational Foundations*, *9*(1), 17–33.

Part II
Lessons Learned in Community Practice, 2005—Ramón Rojano, Guest Editor

Fresh Start for Families: A Collaboratively-built Community-based Program for Families that are Homeless

Peter Fraenkel

Fresh Start for Families is a community-based program for families that are homeless[1] and living in shelters. The core of the program is a nine-week multiple-family discussion group (MFDG) that mixes members' open discussions about challenges and coping approaches with specific activities designed to reverse demoralization, increase hope for a better immediate and long-term future, and revitalize families' resilience. Fresh Start is coordinated with a job-readiness, training, and placement program that parents can elect to join as well as with the shelters housing, childcare, social service, therapy, and recreation resources (see Fig. 1). To date, Fresh Start has been implemented in two New York City shelters: a general family homelessness shelter in the South Bronx housing 212 families and a 52-family shelter for women survivors of domestic violence and their children, whose location is confidential. The families are mostly African-American, Afro-Caribbean, or Latino, mostly headed by single mothers, with children ranging in age from infancy through mid-twenties.

Editors' note: First published in 2005, American Family Therapy Academy Monograph Series.

[1] In keeping with narrative therapy concerns about totalizing labels, we generally avoid the term "homeless families." However, at times sentence structure makes it awkward to use the phrase, "families that are homeless," and we utilize the shorter phrase.

P. Fraenkel (✉)
Center for Work and Family,
Ackerman Institute for the Family, New York, NY, USA
e-mail: pfraenkel@ackerman.org

City University of New York, New York, NY, USA

T. Nelson, H. Winawer (eds.), *Critical Topics in Family Therapy*,
AFTA SpringerBriefs in Family Therapy, DOI 10.1007/978-3-319-03248-1_4,

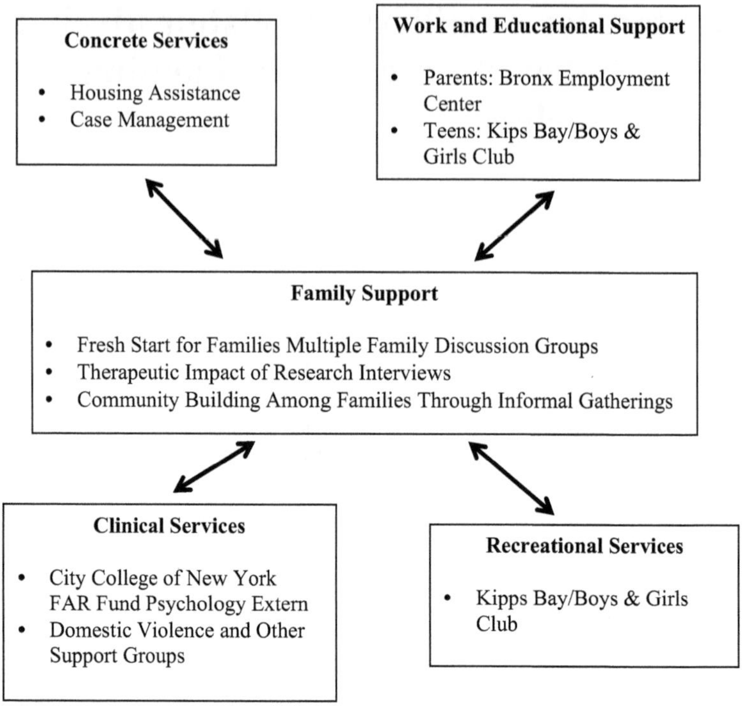

Fig. 1

Fresh Start began in the winter of 1997 in response to the challenges faced by families that were homeless in which unemployed parents were suddenly being forced to move more quickly into the workforce, due to reductions in welfare entitlements following President Clinton's signing of the 1996 Welfare to Work Act. Like many agencies working with poor adults and families, HELP USA, the nation's largest provider of services to the homeless, responded to this law by providing a job- readiness, training, and placement program, but was finding that parents were reluctant to attend or complete this program, or did not stay long in jobs once they obtained them. Tom Hameline, senior vice president of programs and a clinical psychologist trained as a family therapist at the Ackerman Institute, heard a range of concerns expressed by a number of these parents, as well as their employment specialists and case workers, many of which centered on challenges faced by families. Tom sought a consultation from Ackerman, and I [Fraenkel] was asked to work with him; this began a long-term partnership to create systemically based programs for poor families, which is now moving into working with housed families at risk for homelessness. Funding for the program has been through a mixture of federal monies (Housing and Urban Development) and private foundation grants, several of which have represented long-term, sustained support through yearly renewals. Fresh Start was created and continues to be refined and replicated through the use of the collaborative family program development (CFPD) approach (Fraenkel 2003, 2006).

The guiding premise of the CFPD approach is that families, rather than mental health professionals, are the experts on their challenges, their means of coping, and on what they most need in a program. Any program that will consistently engage families—especially those with histories of marginalization and oppression based on race, class, ethnicity, education, and other dimensions of difference—must be built with them as esteemed experts who are offered as much influence in shaping the program as they have time to provide. The ten steps of this approach as they pertained to the creation of Fresh Start are briefly outlined below.

Step 1: Initiating the Project, Forming the Collaborative Professional Relationships, and Engaging Cultural Consultants

Following our initial meetings, Tom and I met with the Bronx regional director of shelter services, the director of the larger family shelter (where we began the program), and the director of social services. All expressed enthusiasm for the idea of a family support program, as did the social services, childcare, recreation, and security staff, employment and housing specialists, and childcare workers when the idea was presented to them in a subsequent meeting. One senior social service staff member was assigned to work with us in coordinating Family interviews and subsequent groups, and was given release time from some of her other responsibilities.

In these initial meetings, we shared professional and personal feelings about the plight of economically marginalized, homeless families, frustrations with attempts to provide service, and fantasies of ideal programs to address the issues. As we each spoke about our experiences and roles with families that are homeless, the diversity in types of expertise and specific concerns emerged, providing us all with a sense of being part of a team, important in alleviating the sense of having to "go it alone" with all the issues presented in the lives of these families. These early meetings, peppered with passionate statements about the larger issues of injustice and social/economic inequity that contribute to homelessness, as well as descriptions of the smaller, daily impediments to aiding these families, were important in building the cohesion and sense of joint purpose that sustained this project for many years despite numerous obstacles.

Patricia Grey, MSW, the shelter director, an Afro-Caribbean-American senior social worker with years of experience working in the shelter system, agreed to serve as a cultural consultant as we shaped the research and program. In addition, at various junctures, I engaged other senior colleagues of color in family research, program development, and therapy as cultural consultants, including Carmen Rodriguez, PhD, Kenneth Hardy, PhD, Paulette Hines, PhD, and Vanessa Clover, MSW, the director of the domestic violence shelter. I also had the opportunity to ask Nancy Boyd- Franklin, PhD, to evaluate the program in her role as a discussant during a presentation at a Multicultural Institute conference. Engaging senior colleagues as cultural consultants was especially important given that both Tom and I are white middle-class males who have never been homeless.

Step 2: Intensive Interviewing of Family Members

Families are interviewed extensively for up to four hours with breaks, snacks, dinner, and a small monetary stipend. Although we were initially anxious that families would fatigue midway through the interview, we found repeatedly that they seemed instead to become even more energized as the interview went on: they smiled more, told more elaborated anecdotes, and family members interacted more freely with one another. They often confused the interview with the support program itself. Families explained that this interview was the first time anyone had taken an interest in their story and asked them not only about their difficulties but how they had coped. Most of the interviews they had experienced in social service settings had focused on what they weren't doing or didn't have—jobs, homes, savings—and seemed implicitly and sometimes, explicitly to blame them for these circumstances. They also appreciated being asked to contribute ideas to the program. As one woman stated, "Most programs just tell us things we already know. But you listened. Sometimes, people just have to listen to us."

Step 3: Intensive Interviewing of Agency Professionals

In addition to the previously described preliminary meetings of professionals that are focused on team-building, we interviewed front-line professionals in depth to hear their observations and beliefs about families' challenges and coping methods, professionals' own challenges and coping methods in attempting to do their jobs with overwhelming caseloads and little time or resources, and the professionals' recommendations for the program. We conducted these professional interviews only after first interviewing several families because we wanted our experience of their lives to be shaped first by the families. In many instances, group interviews with staff professionals led them to new and more empathic understandings of family member behavior that workers previously attributed to "bad attitudes," "laziness," and "uncooperativeness."

Step 4: Phrase-By-Phrase Qualitative Coding

Families' video- or audio-taped interviews were qualitatively coded sentence by sentence by me and a multiracial team of graduate students in order to identify themes of challenge, coping, and program recommendations. Although time-consuming (it takes about two hours to code five minutes of tape), we believe the unique voice and wisdom of each family can only be captured by slowing down our listening process.

Step 5: Creating Program Formats and Contents and Writing an Initial Manual

Families' suggestions for the program, as well as shelter workers' recommendations, guided everything from when, how long, and how often during the course of the week the groups met; whether to have parents and kids together always or separate for some of the time; what to do when members didn't attend; and what activities to include. Although there are differences among the three versions of Fresh Start, and differences across the nine weeks of the MFDG, all versions proceeded through the following sequence: dinner, greetings and announcements, work (or school) progress reports that highlighted even small positive changes and sources of pride, families' presentations of what they did with home activities suggested at the end of the previous week's group, discussion of challenges and sharing of coping approaches, and presentation of the next week's home activities. Home activities included an exercise in externalizing homelessness; discussing each family members' "dream jobs;" creating a one-year timeline of the family's goals; a collage or mobile of challenges and coping approaches using magazine photos, index cards, and drawings; using arts and crafts supplies to create masks that depicted—metaphorically speaking—the "face" a battered woman shows the world to hide her fear; and families writing letters of appreciation to themselves from five years in the future that make meaning of the present and emphasize their resilience.

We also created a Card Sort activity that provided a direct link between the research and the program, as well as adding some structure to the discussion of challenges and coping. Each challenge mentioned in a family interview was written on a card and in the group, families were asked to sort the total set of cards into three categories in terms of relevance to them: (I) Not at All a Challenge, (II) Somewhat of a Challenge, and (III) Definitely a Challenge. Family members were then asked to begin by picking one card from Category I that they would like to share with the group. Of course, what one family finds not challenging another family might find somewhat or definitely a challenge, and this provided opportunities for one family to help another.

The program is specified in a manual (Fraenkel and Shannon 1999) so that it could be disseminated and conducted by front-line workers who might not have much experience conducting group or family therapy or community programs.

Step 6: Piloting of the Group with Meeting-By-Meeting Evaluations by Participants

At the end of each group meeting, members filled out a short questionnaire to evaluate that meeting. They were asked to write a sentence in answer to the question, "What was the most important thing that happened or was said today?" They also rated the degree of helpfulness of the meeting, and noted anything they did not like about the meeting. We made a commitment to rectify anything they did not like by the next meeting, or at least present it to the group for discussion at the next meeting.

Step 7: Revising the Program and Manual

Each new family interview and each new group provided opportunities to alter the program and manual. Thus, the manual was not a rigid, unchanging document, but reflected ongoing collaboration between families and program developers.

Step 8: Intensive Interviewing of Families for Each Subsequent Group Cycle

One difference between the CFPD approach and typical needs assessments is that, even though we by then had interviewed 250 families, conducted 35 cycles of the nine-week program, and written manuals for three versions of it (families with young children, families with teens, families that survived domestic violence), each new family joining the program was first interviewed, and the experiences and ideas shared were incorporated into program materials. Thus, program development was ongoing and all families had the opportunity to experience themselves as experts. Ongoing in-depth interviewing of families also allowed us to keep abreast of changes in city, state, and federal laws and policies that affect poor families and our program, as families often experience the ramifications of these changes before they become widely known to social service providers or the news media.

Step 9: Evaluating Effectiveness in Comparison or Randomized Designs

Following the interviews, we gave each family a packet of self-report measures that assess degree of well-being on the individual, family, and family-in-community levels. With parents' permission, we also obtained progress reports from the employment program. Following completion of the program, and when possible, at six-month and one-year follow-up points, we re-administered these research instruments.

[By the time of the writing of this chapter], we had conducted evaluation of Fresh Start without a formal control group—an appropriate design for the first stage in developing an intervention. However, we embarked on the first randomized evaluation that would compare Fresh Start to the existing programs provided in the shelter that do not offer a specific family format or focus (a teen recreation group and a group for parents that provides opportunities to discuss problems in shelter life). These existing programs along with parenting and money management classes are typical offerings in family shelters.

Step 10: Disseminating and Adapting the Program to Other Settings

We began Fresh Start at the general Family shelter, developed a version for families that survived domestic violence, and then returned to the general shelter to develop a new program for families with teens. We sent manuals to various agencies in the U.S.—including those working with families displaced by Hurricane Katrina—as well as abroad. We also developed a training program for front-line professionals.

Has the Program Helped Anyone?

As noted, we are engaging in both qualitative and quantitative evaluations to determine detailed answers to this question. Data analyses conducted so far are quite supportive, including

- Significant decreases for adults in demoralization as measured by the PERI Demoralization Index (Dohrenwend et al. 1980) and psychological symptoms as measured by the Symptom Checklist-90-Revised (SCL-90-R; Derogatis n.d.), and for kids, decreases on level of child behavior problems as measured by the Child Behavior Checklist (CBCL; Achenbach 1991).[2]
- Consistently high ratings of the helpfulness of group meetings by family members (average rating of 4.57 on a 5-point helpfulness scale).
- Higher rates of engagement in the job-readiness program and in employment than for adults who did not participate in the program.
- Higher rates of engagement in Fresh Start than in other programs offered at the shelter such as on parenting and programs for teens.

[2] The PERI Demoralization Index, SCL-90-R, and CBCL are all widely used measures of psychological and behavioral difficulties. Scale references are available from the author on request.

Challenges

There were a few challenges we faced:

Lack of Time

All staff members of the project had many other commitments. But by keeping regular times for the program and research, it was embedded in our schedules, and became part of our weekly routines. Yet we always felt we could spend much more time on the project.

Pressure on Families to Move Out

Over the years, the pressure for families to be placed in permanent housing was increased by the city government, leading families to be increasingly reluctant to commit to the program even though their average length of stay had actually stayed the same. We adapted by creating shorter versions of the program, such as a four-hour version held once on a weekend.

Changes in Welfare and Housing Policies

One of our most important outcome measures was whether parents obtained employment. Yet two years [before the writing of this article], the city changed its policies so that if parents obtained a job before placement in subsidized housing, they were immediately disqualified from receiving such housing. We sided with the parents, encouraging them to complete all the steps up to getting a job (completing job-readiness and training) and to wait until obtaining housing before getting a job (Fraenkel et al. 2005).

Why Do We Keep Doing It?

This work has been the most moving in my life, a feeling shared by my students and many other professionals who have worked with us. The families we met truly are an inspiration—although we arrived at the shelter each week already exhausted, we left reinvigorated. And we kept doing it because we promised Diane, one of the first women to participate in the groups. In a six-month follow- up interview, she said, “Don’t give up on the people, because you’ll have another group like us. What made the difference was that you all didn't treat us like we were clients and you were workers. You treated us like we were friends, and that's what made the difference."

Acknowledgement This program and research were supported by grants from the Louis and Anne Abrons Foundation, the Altria Doors of Hope Program, the Francis L. and Edwin L. Cummings Memorial Fund, the Ruth Perl Kahn Research Fund, the Dorothea L. Leonhardt Foundation, and HELP USA.

References

Achenbach, T. M. (1991). *Manual for the child behavior checklist/4-18 and 1991 Profile*. Burlington, VT: University of Vermont Department of Psychiatry.

Derogatis, L. R. (n.d.). *The symptom checklist-90-revised*. Pearson Assessments. www.pearsonassessments@pearson.com.

Dohrenwend, B. P., Shrout, P.E., Egri, G., & Mendelsohn, F.S. (1980). Nonspecific psychological distress and other dimensions of psychopathology. *Archives of General Psychiatry, 37*, 1229–1238.

Fraenkel, P., & Shannon, M. (1999). *Multiple family discussion group manual: Family support from welfare to work program (Fresh Start for Families)*. New York, NY: Ackerman Institute for the Family.

Fraenkel, P. (2003, June). *Learning from the experts: Research-based collaborative program development with marginalized families*. Plenary address, 25th Annual Meeting of the American Family Therapy Academy, Miami, Florida.

Fraenkel, P., Hameline, T., & Kowal, S. (2005, June). *Societal, institutional, and personal politics in the life of a community-based family program for domestic survivors in transition from welfare to work*. Paper presented at the IFTA International Conference on Family therapy, Washington, D.C.

Fraenkel, P. (2006). Engaging families as experts: Collaborative family program development. *Family Process, 45*, 237–257.

Systemic Community Psychiatry

Marcelo Pakman

On different occasions I have written about the integration of systemic approaches in community mental health. They have included experiences of constructive therapies in day treatment and outpatient settings (Pakman 1999), a thorough analysis of the state of the mental health system in community settings (Pakman 2003), and a risk-reduction program for multiproblem families (Pakman 2007). Having elaborated on attempts at impacting the delivery of mental health services with the introduction of systemic practices, I want to introduce a preliminary account of my work as a systemically oriented community psychiatrist, based on my experience since my arrival in the U.S. in 1989 at the beginning of the managed care era.

In the current mental health system, credentials are destiny. As psychiatrists (physicians), our work in community mental health settings is necessarily restricted to providing psychiatric services, which has come to mean so-called "medication management." Psychotherapy is generally provided by other professionals (social workers, psychologists, nurses, and educational specialists) to those same clients whose purported "chemical imbalances" (a term increasingly in use by mental health practitioners in the current "decade of the brain"). Still, well paid within the hierarchy of the mental health services system, psychiatrists saw their expertise increasingly constrained by a rather limited biological view and their practice restricted to serving as "neurotransmitter technicians." The new generation of psychiatrists, trained only on this simplistic biological view of emotional problems, does not have adequate knowledge about psychotherapy; training and expertise in the social aspects of mental illness has all but disappeared for them.

Editors' note: First published in 2005, American Family Therapy Academy Monograph Series.

Editors' note: Although this chapter was written in 2005, we see little change from Dr. Pakman's assertions about so-called "modern" psychiatry and the lack of systemic or poststructural approaches within psychiatry.

M. Pakman (✉)
Springfield, MA, USA
e-mail: mpakman@gmail.com

T. Nelson, H. Winawer (eds.), *Critical Topics in Family Therapy*,
AFTA SpringerBriefs in Family Therapy, DOI 10.1007/978-3-319-03248-1_5,

Faced with this situation, mental health professionals like myself, who graduated in the politically heated environment of Latin America in the 1970s with a view of psychiatrists as intellectuals at the crossroads of the social, the psychological, and the biological, have had to put our systemic minds and skills to work. I have been working with poor populations in Massachusetts, whose healthcare needs are usually covered by basic government health insurance in outpatient and day treatment program settings. Minorities (predominantly Latinos and Blacks) are largely represented and clients usually present with complex, compounding health conditions.

Here we have a Decalogue of some of the lessons learned:

- It is impossible to integrate the biological and the psychological in mental health if we try to put together a simplistic and individually based view of biology with an individually based, nonsystemic, and decontextualized view of the mind and of psychotherapy.
- As a psychiatrist, in order to go beyond the language of neurotransmitters and chemical imbalances, a common model of treatment is needed, along with a language more suited to move elegantly among those fields without stretching concepts beyond coherence. The premises of Batesonian systemic thinking and cybernetics, as well as postmodernist and poststructuralist literature, provide a solid basis for such a language and methodology.
- The implementation of this common language and methodology is facilitated when we focus on what different mental health professionals do in practice, beyond their abstract theoretical allegiances (Schön 1983, 1991). This is a way to go beyond the conundrum of how different professionals with different theoretical approaches can work with the same clients.
- The interventions of any professional join other cultural influences to become "objects-in-use" (Rein and Schön 1994), open to reframing, redefinition and transformations under the impact of further interventions. This allows us to work on the way clients use therapeutic interventions in connection with psychopharmacological interventions.
- Psychotherapeutic interventions are always implemented by sociosomatic organisms, and all somatic interventions happen as social acts (medicating is a social act). During psychiatric visits, as they are implemented now, the usual theme of conversation is called "medication." However, the meaning of this theme, its impact on the social and psychological goals of care, and its role in terms of the client's interactions can all become legitimate subjects of therapeutic conversation.
- In the drama of individually based symptoms, the role of medication as a life event must be an integral part of the systemic view. A central focus for us is the role of symptom change in achieving therapy goals. Further, we focus on the politics of medication use in the mental health hierarchy and the position of the mental health program in the community.
- The participation of family and network members in consultations can be used as a complement to medication as a factor in life events without necessarily assuming a traditional family therapy approach, which we, as psychiatrists, have not been legitimized to do officially.

- An essential part of our systemic work is a careful negotiation with each client (and family) regarding what to expect from psychopharmacological interventions and a discussion about the relationship that the medication has with the client and his/her family or social network (including other providers). We also discuss the client's own evaluation of target symptoms. Constant use of evaluation and consideration of multiple perspectives and expectations is essential.
- Systemic community psychiatry is the art of managing the micropolitics of sociosomatic situations. The client, the social network, the family, mental health system actors, and we (psychiatrist consultants?) are all part of that complex dynamic in which simple interventions can trigger cascades of positive amplifying events. In this light, we take medications (just as we might with nutrition, level of physical activity, lifestyle preferences, etc.) as a way of "calibrating" the nervous system in a way that is more or less conducive to the types of goals clients establish for themselves. I claim that an integration of biologically oriented psychiatry with the larger mental health system, along with use of systemic methodologies and language, also facilitates integration of mental health and primary care.
- We advise making systemic language "invisible" to conversations in meetings to avoid conveying that we are trying to impose a "different" approach and to avoid ideological struggles. Open confrontation should be used only occasionally when we consider there are unethical practices. Nevertheless, we have to relentlessly practice always taking a metastance instead of direct confrontation. I prefer language that sounds similar to traditional medical language to interact with colleagues and patients, since it enables colleagues and clients to take in the information they expect along with the systemic message I seek to impart. In community mental health settings not connected with academia, it is, in my experience, more effective to "hide" within this invisible program the richness of practice that systemic thinking offers.

References

Pakman, M. (1999). Designing constructive therapies in community mental health: Poetics and micro-politics in and beyond the consulting room. *Journal of Marital and Family Therapy, 25*, 83–98.

Pakman, M. (2003). A systemic frame for mental health practices. In P. S. Proski & D. V. Keith (Eds.), *Family therapy as an alternative to medication: An appraisal of farmland* (pp. 93–110). New York, NY: Brunner-Routledge.

Pakman, M. (2007). Risk reduction in multiproblem families: The micro-politics of social justice in mental healthcare. In E. Aldarondo (Ed.), *Promoting social justice through mental health practice* (pp. 151–173). New York, NY: Lawrence Erlbaum Associates.

Rein, M. & Schön, D. (1994). *Frame reflection: Toward the resolution of intractable policy controversies*. New York, NY: Basic Books.

Schön, D. (1983). *The reflective practitioner*. New York, NY: Basic Books.

Schön, D. (Ed.). (1991). *The reflective turn: Case studies in and on educational practice*. New York, NY: Teachers College, Columbia University.

Constructing Empowerment and Resilience Contexts: Systemic Interventions in Communities

Rosa Maria Stefanini de Macedo

> The utopian is not the unrealizable. The utopia is not the idealism…
> But is to denounce the inhumanity of the structures and to announce their humanity.
> That is the reason why utopia is also an historic compromise.…Paulo Freire, 1987, *Pedagogia de oprimído*

One of the major problems in Brazil is unfair income distribution. Statistical data show that the wealthy, a group of 1.8 million, comprise 50 % of Brazil's wealth while the other 50 % is distributed among 178 million people. This enormous gap between classes has severe social consequences, chief among which is social and economic inequality. Nearly one-third of the population lives in poverty, which means they have a less than minimum salary[1] per month (100 $). One-third of Brazilians live below the poverty line, earning 3 $ a month or less. They face economic, educational, and cultural barriers, which create an environment of exclusion and prejudice.

Our past research (Macedo and Saleh 2001) has supported Foucault's (1979) tenet that people in such contexts become "docile bodies," living through daily hardship and suffering as if this is "natural." Many of the poor cannot be assisted by the overburdened Welfare Services system. Public programs in health and education are very expensive in Brazil, as in other developing countries around the world. Further, each time the government needs more money, the welfare budget is reduced. So, the financial aid that public institutions and private social clinics target for the poor is chronically insufficient. When families succeed in getting those services, they wait so long for an appointment that frequently it becomes purposeless. It is common to

[1] In Brazil, the minimum salary is the least amount an employer can pay to an employee by federal law.

Editors' note: First published in 2005, American Family Therapy Academy Monograph Series.

R. M. S. de Macedo (✉)
Pontifical Catholic University of São Paulo, São Paulo, Brazil
e-mail: romacedo@pucsp.br

T. Nelson, H. Winawer (eds.), *Critical Topics in Family Therapy*,
AFTA SpringerBriefs in Family Therapy, DOI 10.1007/978-3-319-03248-1_6,

see both professionals and institutions burned out and numbed by the pressure of public demand and chronic shortfall of assistance.

As family researchers and therapists committed to ethics in relationships, we are sensitized to the problem of inequality and the challenges it represents. At our agency, Nucleus for Family and Community (NUFAC—PUCSP), we felt that we could not remain indifferent to the ethical and social justice questions in our clinical work. We agreed that it was necessary to break down the boundaries of traditional psychology practice, and to movc toward bringing it to the community including schools, churches, clubs, nongovernmental organizations, and even public meeting spaces such as parks and squares.

Our model is based on the work of authors with culturally sensitive practices in community settings, such as Freire (1987), Minuchin and Colapinto (1998), Stephens et al. (1997), Waldegrave (1990), Dabas and Najmanovich (1995), Bárreto (2005), Macedo (1986), Macedo and Saleh (2001), and Grandesso (2000). These authors all affirm that the experience of chronic frustration and deprivation creates feelings of powerlessness and a belief in the incapacity of managing one's own life. Therapists must consider the context of social, political, and economic exclusion as a prime factor in the development of psychological problems and suffering.

In the formative years of NUFAC, we were a group of eight doctoral clinical psychologists specializing in family therapy, professors in the graduate training program at the Pontifical Catholic University of Sao Paulo, Brazil. Over time, the group expanded to include affiliated professors from other universities, undergraduate and graduate students, and externs in family and community therapy. We knew that we would need to begin by understanding how families living in the greatest poverty handle the stressors of their everyday lives, as well as their beliefs, lifestyles, challenges, and hopes. Our goals in creating NUFAC have been to (a) deconstruct and challenge stereotypes and myths about families living in poverty; (b) identify family strengths, promote members' self-identification as citizens with rights and abilities, and strengthen resilience in the face of adversity; (c) teach healthcare and social science professionals a competence focus in order to serve the families more effectively; and (d) sensitize our public health system to the importance of implementing better public policies and programs for the families.

NUFAC's research and clinical work is based on the constructivist model, i.e., the world of meanings as "constructed" by the observer. We assume a nonhierarchical position with the families and community members we plan to serve. Our clinical interventions are narrative techniques, developing goals, and creating change in dialogue with community groups based on their life experiences and their ideas (Freedman and Combs 1996; White and Epston 1999). We also have used group techniques such as role-playing, sculpting, and some other nonverbal techniques to enhance therapeutic conversation. The larger purpose of the agency is to develop alternative approaches that will allow creative intervention with a large number of individuals and families within their home communities. During the past 5 years we also began to adopt principles from the System Integrative Model for Community Therapy. This approach was created by Adalberto Barreto (2005), a psychiatrist and anthropologist who sees human suffering as the central organizer of therapeutic conversation. The objectives of System Integrative therapy are (a) to promote social networking and experiential exchange among participants; (b) to emphasize competence, improve self-esteem, and facilitate self-empowerment; and (c) to develop "another story" of clients' lives in which problems are redefined (Barreto 2005; Grandesso 2005). This model of therapy demands study about larger systems, since communities are unpredictable and complex human systems.

Our project began in 1989 and was developed in four stages: (a) research interviews with families about their needs and concerns; (b) reflexive conversation family groups, in which families share their experiences with one another; (c) focus groups to discuss the special themes and problems that emerged from the research interviews and reflexive conversation groups; (d) training groups and workshops to target specific populations such as parent groups, teacher groups, and healthcare provider/service provider groups; and (e) open community therapy groups for members of the community.

Our Program

Reflexive Groups and Focus Groups

These are offered to parents with sons or daughters enrolled in social programs at nongovernmental agencies or schools in the community, parish members, public school teachers, public health professionals, and agency workers (healthcare professionals at all levels of administration are combined together).

Training Workshops. Professional workshops and practical exercises address problems and teach skills needed for childrearing, educational interventions for students, and family structure-family intervention. These are targeted to parents, teachers, community aid workers, and social service workers.

Community Therapy

Large numbers of people from local communities meet in an open group. Groups are held in public spaces easily accessible such as hospitals, churches, and childcare buildings. Each session becomes a self-contained, single therapeutic experience to all the participants who are present that day. The meetings do not require a continuous commitment as does traditional therapy. However, when a client attends multiple community therapy meetings over a period of time, the intervention is transformed into a long-term therapeutic process (Grandesso 2005). Each session is structured in stages: (a) welcome and warming; (b) selecting the theme; (c) contextualization (naming and understanding suffering); (d) group sharing; and (e) closing rituals. These are heterogeneous groups because within one community, therapy session participants range in age and come from diverse social, economic, and cultural settings.

A great variety of themes may be worked depending on the needs presented in each group, for example, alcoholism, domestic violence, depression, or abandonment. However, typically, one to two themes are selected for each session, and a member is chosen to present his/her problem. Everyone participates in sharing experiences, singing popular songs that are reflective of the themes that emerge, and discussing the comments of the day's presenter. The therapist functions as a facilitator. To open the reflexive group conversation, s/he identifies the problem, which is called a "mote" for that group meeting. The presenting member makes his or her comments and thus begins the conversation about the chosen problem.

During the contextualization stage, the therapist opens up dialogue by inviting the other attendees to discuss the mote together. For example, the mote may be alcoholism. After listening to the presenter's narrative about how the alcohol has created distress for him/her and the family, the therapist asks, "Who has experienced a situation like this one? Who has felt like the one who is presenting here today?" Each participant has an opportunity to connect with the mote (theme).

The reflexive dialogue creates time to reflect about mutual experience, to revise members' view of the problem, to identify resources and competences, and to share learning with the others. In this approach, each dialogue is culturally rooted in the themes that emerge from the participants, in their own language, and their own way of understanding their experiences.

Violence, substance abuse, couple infidelity, robbery, gang disputes, sexual abuse, divorce, abandonment, and many other kinds of complaints are presented. Sometimes a person or family needs to be referred to individual therapy or to a specialized provider (e.g., psychiatrist, primary care physician). The therapist is expected to know the resources in each community served, and to be in contact with its other systems as an integral part of the program. In our model, fortifying provider networks at the professional level is as important for success as is fortifying the network among members of each community.

As a result of our project, many changes have been observed within the communities where we hold group meetings. For example, in our evaluation of the changes in parent attitudes and behaviors, we have observed:

- Increased strengthening of primary affection bonds and visioning of home as a privileged place for raising and caring for children.
- Improved flexibility in authoritative and rigid patterns of discipline and increased ability to negotiate with sons and daughters.
- A disposition to learn and participate more in community social projects, in child and adolescent development, and in understanding the problems in intergenerational relationships in the phases of the life cycle.
- Development of solidarity and reciprocity with other parents of the neighborhood to share concerns about monitoring and guiding children.
- Strengthening of investment in children by directing them toward studying when possible instead of/in addition to working for earnings.

- Improvement of the relationship between parent and school and more attention to the school problems faced by children.

Testimonies that we received from families regarding this project included statements such as the following: "…today I've learned a very important thing: my son has grown and is changing…he is gaining more autonomy…. I have learned today that I have to act differently…. I have to stop yelling, shouting; to show limits and self-control as an example for them…." "I have learned that we have to be self-confident and not underestimate ourselves about our capacity to educate them…." "I discovered a way of having peace at home: instead of fighting against my daughter to do her homework, I gave her space in the kitchen table and I stay near, cooking the lunch, while she studies, so I keep calm and all… things go better."

Through delivery of the community therapy program, we have also observed a change in group dynamics. The relationship among community members creates a sheltering and warm connection. There is more availability and respect for someone else's suffering. Members experience more generosity in giving and also receiving support. They come to recognize that each one learns from the other. We have also observed a mutual view taking form among members that legitimates differences and recognizes the competencies of each individual. This view recognizes each person in the group as legitimate honorable others, respecting their cultural values and the wisdom they have developed through life experience. As a consequence it promotes resilience, which we at NUFAC define as the ability to transform challenges into growth and autonomy through the development and promotion of social and support networks.

There are many challenges, including lack of public investment in health and education, lack of money to meet the needs, and mistrust in new communities regarding the objectives of our program. We also have to address the doubts that public agencies, the local people, and even some professionals show about the possibility of change. Mental health and healthcare professionals also have to struggle against fear of the drug dealers, the "parallel power" that controls our slums. Dealers frequently threaten professionals and families with expulsion (exile), injury, or death if they disclose information regarding drug-related "business." Yet the increasing involvement of health professionals from the public service and private clinics with this program has been very effective in galvanizing some authorities to introduce and develop similar ventures within the welfare system. Therapists in the welfare system are particularly enthusiastic about our intervention model because this way of working diminishes waiting lists. Our trainees and supervisees believe in just therapy, and feel themselves useful to a greater number of people with this model of practice.

What motivates us to continue this work is the strong feeling and consciousness of being able to contribute to the inclusion of people into social benefits they deserve as citizens. We are conscious also that we help them to improve their self-esteem, self-confidence, empowerment, and resilience. As a result, I believe that all professionals and volunteers involved are "constructing" a society with more justice, hope, and humanity.

References

Bárreto, A. P. (2005). *Terapia comunitária passo a passo*. Fortaleza, Brazil: A. P. Barreto.

Dabas, E., & Najmanovich, D. (1995). *Redes: El lenguaje de los vínculos*. Buenos Aires, Argentina: Paídos.

Foucault, M. (1979). *Microfisica do poder*. Rio de Janeiro, Brazil: Graal.

Freedman, J., & Combs, G. (1996). *Narrative therapy: The social construction of preferred realities*. New York, NY: Norton.

Freire, P. (1987). *Pedagogia do oprimído*. Rio de Janeiro, Brazil: Paz e Terra.

Grandesso, M. (2000). *Terapia ejustiça social: Questões de dor em terapia familiar*. São Paulo, Brazil: APTF.

Grandesso, M. (2005, June). *Community therapy: a context of empowerment and resilience*. Presented at AFTA-IFTA International Conference on Family Therapy, Washington, D.C., U.S.

Macedo, R. M. S. (1986). Psicologia e instituição; Novas formas de atendimento. São Paulo, Brazil: Cortez.

Macedo, R. M. S., & Saleh, L. R. P. (2001). Famílias em Contexto de Pobreza. Unpublished Master's Thesis, Pontifical Catholic University of São Palo, São Palo, Brazil.

Minuchin, P., & Colapinto, J. (1998). *Working with families of the poor*. New York, NY: Guilford Press.

Stephens, R., Waldegrave, C., & Frater, P. (1997). An overview of research on poverty in New Zealand. *New Zealand Sociology*, *12*, 213–259.

Waldegrave, C. (1990). Just therapy. *Dulwiche Centre Newsletter*, *1*, 5–46. Australia.

White, M., & Epston, D. (1999). *Narrative means to therapeutic ends*. New York, NY: Norton.

Challenges and Changes to Family Therapy Practice in South Africa

Madhubala Ishver Kasiram and Emmerentie Oliphant

Family therapy in South Africa seriously challenges traditional theoretical paradigms as we struggle with horrific crime and violence at family and political levels. This paper examines published work modifying family therapy practice in South Africa since 1988. Whilst undertaking this exercise, it was interesting to observe the allegiance South African clinicians had to their international counterparts by using international models, language, and theory to understand, articulate, and test modifications. We propose in this paper that we need not confine ourselves to this mold and should be bold in charting new territories in family therapy. We must confidently embrace our own forms of theory and intervention. This paper addresses challenges facing South African family therapists and resulting changes, which have enlivened and shaped family therapy for local and perhaps international consumption. Central to our work are innovations in several areas: (a) how our practice accommodates "difference"; (b) how we embrace "community"; and (c) how we use nature, drama, and the arts to creatively engage with families.

The Challenges

Our unique context and need for special understanding emerged as early as 1988 during the 4th National Conference of the South African Institute of Marital and Family Therapy. At this meeting practitioners spoke of practicing "Western-style" family therapy in Soweto amid poverty and hopelessness (Nell and Seedat 1988). So many of our couples and families suffer from poverty, oppression, disempowerment,

---

Editors' note: First published in 2005, American Family Therapy Academy Monograph Series.

M. I. Kasiram (✉)
School of Applied Human Sciences, University of KwaZulu Natal, Durban, South Africa
e-mail: kasiramm@ukzn.ac.za

E. Oliphant
Stephen F. Austin State University, Nacogdoches, TX, USA

T. Nelson, H. Winawer (eds.), *Critical Topics in Family Therapy*,
AFTA SpringerBriefs in Family Therapy, DOI 10.1007/978-3-319-03248-1_7,

and despair; rather than choosing either a macro-view or a micro-, within-family view, they suggested working with both. Lifschitz (1988) also invited therapists to take "psychotherapeutic contexts" to Black families by seeing the world through their eyes rather than Western-tinted lenses. He referred to appreciating rituals of African religion and practices to co-create new context-relevant therapies for South African family therapists.

The South African context warrants deviation from traditional systemic interventions. Both South African family therapists as well as those practicing in the western world among deprived communities appear to appreciate the need for freedom from the mold. Some refer to the American "myth" of a melting pot of cultures and communities that apparently blend harmoniously, emphasizing that in reality, there is no such blending and suggesting a need to co-evolve with context. Clearly, there is need for freedom from dominating influences to create culture-sensitive practice. Morkel (2004), a South African writer, has gone so far as to state that she has felt "handicapped" by "professional training and the isolated, privileged life I lead as a White South African," commenting that training failed her in respectfully reaching disadvantaged communities.

Kasiram (2000) has discussed therapeutic "failure" as perceived resistance to therapy. She asks whether it is the family that is failing to respond, or the therapist that is failing the family. Disadvantaged communities pose the challenge to examine such "failings."

McNamee (2004) refers to how "consistency is admired" (p. 225) when we should rather be creative when our learned theories are not relevant or effective in application. For example, Hall (2000) discusses Zimbabwean families whose members have been wiped out by AIDS. She has found that traditional casework and family therapy are not useful for these families facing catastrophic illness and loss, and advises that creativity, humility, and humanity are crucial tools in searching for indigenous models of practice. Finally, Rundell (2000) expresses frustration with traditional supervisory methods when working within financial and human support constraints. Rundell advocates a model of therapists in training and client communities as "co-visionaries" in their own growth and change-producing events (p. 150).

Respect for Difference

"Difference" has so many guises in the family therapy context. McDowell et al. (2002) refer to developing a culture of "pluralism" where "multiple perspectives are cultivated and valued" (p. 180). The key is to practice family therapy "in the moment" (McNamee 2004, p. 224), where we give credence to ways of life and being, and respect that which is different from the dominant culture. This may mean redefining "family" to capture its various faces, especially in South Africa where we have so many child-headed households where parents have died of AIDS. We also need to affirm the strength of these family structures, and deviate from promoting the autonomy and individuation of systems and individuals when there is community catastrophe. Indeed, many therapists have referred to the family as "expert," managing and controlling their circumstances via an array of supports and structures that we could not imagine possible. In this vein, Kasiram and Partab (2002) refer to the power of the family and community in facilitating grieving when a nation experiences multiple losses.

A further difference to be respected is that in many financially constrained families, male members do not avail themselves for therapy, a feature also noted by Bean et al. (2002). Sliep (2000) also has commented on her decision to work with female family members who needed to tell their stories of courage in facing AIDS. Although she found that the men were not ready to use prevention services or participate in therapy, the women were prepared to fight the horror of AIDS and take precautions to save their children even if it seemed to be too late.

There are linguistic differences that force us to be culturally appropriate. Ajila (2004) discussed the use of proverbs, prayers, and names amongst the Yoruba in Nigeria, Africa as adjuncts to therapy. Neurolinguistics is being recognized as a force controlling behavior, since it is derived from culture and values. Sliep (2000), for example, used the axiom that the stick in a bundle is stronger than when it is isolated, to help women afflicted with AIDS to come together to search for solutions. Says Ajila (2004), names bearing the word "akin," meaning fearless, could be employed in therapeutic conversations to re-introduce the fighting spirit in the individual or family. Jeewa (2005) discusses how language can disempower persons who have abused drugs by referring to them as "recovering addicts" who must be constantly on guard should they fall prey to a past. Instead, he suggests they be praised for breaking free and could regard themselves as being "cured." A new language introduces a fresh frame of reference against which future change and progress may be plotted and valued. So, searching for culturally specific language that will achieve these ends becomes a process goal that pervades our therapy.

Another type of linguistic intervention that we use comes through the use of "cultural metaphors" such as the "trickster" in African-American communities. The "trickster" has weaved himself into the life of the family to make life difficult. Using the concept of the trickster in therapy allows distance between the problem and the people, a concept similar to externalization within the narrative therapy framework (Akinyela 2004).

Difference in the form of dissonance among generations within a family also is an issue that challenges therapists to practice outside of the box. Lee and Mjelde-Mossey (2004) argue for using multiple sets of values even when they are seemingly conflicted. Such dissonance occurs all too easily because of different responses by generational groups within a family to mass media portrayal of dominant cultures. Family members are often at varying levels of acceptance or rejection of dominant influences and these become the agenda for negotiation when therapists recognize the effect of such dissonance. In this light, Barnard (2004) refers to how traditional foundations in South Africa are hurt and disintegrate in the face of modern values and moral codes of conduct. Winfield and students (2004) use role play to hear these multiple perspectives within families and communities in order to restore relationships and promote social harmony. Morkel (2004) also demonstrates the disillusionment parents experience when their children adopt values different from theirs. She uses the metaphor of "rites of passage" from a narrative perspective to bring together dissenting voices to create understanding and harmony.

Respecting difference may mean getting in touch with our cultural roots to experience liberation from materialism, where love, enjoyment, and laughter are considered indicators of "success" and happiness. We appear to have accepted and become trapped by a world that is achievement oriented. We are no longer human "be-ings" but human "do-ings," taking no time for ourselves or simple pleasures. Perhaps traditional villages and peoples that celebrate happiness or living through dance and song, sharing a smoke, or taking time out to just "be" need to guide us again, so that we may be less wearied by the world. These differences ought to be highlighted.

Community Responsiveness

Many therapists/researchers acknowledge the ever-present and powerful context of community. McDowell et al. (2002) ask that we transform by increasing "awareness of the systems of privilege and oppression that define equity and justice" (p. 180). Oliphant (2005) suggests that empowerment and uplifting of communities through the use of developmental strategies must complement microsystemic strategies such as those of family interventions. Rojano (2005) agrees that family therapists combine family therapy with developmental and motivational theories, community mental health, economic development, and community mobilization strategies. Hernandez et al. (2005) mention the need for intervening at the intersection between family and community. They challenge family therapists to continue in the tradition of being leaders that produce cutting-edge thinkers, and invite us to critically engage in the process of allying with the community in this regard. Bean et al. (2002) cautions that a past steeped in social injustice and discrimination makes some families wary and even distrusting of therapists.

How do we translate these ideals into practical reality? In realizing that individual therapy could not address families that were rebuilding after traumatic loss, Petty (2004) trained a group of kinship caretakers to act as therapeutic agents in their children's lives. This was an empowerment strategy to sustain not one, but many families simultaneously. When community members are taught to develop their consciousnesses about community issues, they take collective action and reaffirm their collective strength (Nair 2004). However, one must not underestimate the difficulties in promoting collective action to address sociopolitical problems.

Indeed, the model of "community family therapy" proposed by Rojano (2005) offers to unravel some of these difficulties. A central tenet of his model, accessing community resources for sustaining growth, is mentioned along with leadership development and civic engagement. The reality is that apathy is often the hallmark of disenfranchised communities, and in order to begin the process of consciousness-raising, this trend needs to be broken. Naidoo and Kasiram (2003) agree, however, that "office-bound," quick fixes via microsystemic familytherapy interventions are a good deal easier than the long-term slog of connecting meaningfully with communities.

Office-bound microsystemic interventions are clearly no longer relevant as we enter an era of recognizing and valuing community. For example, in discussing issues of gender and equality, Hernandez et al. (2005) discussed the formation of "culture circles" to raise critical consciousness. However, they challenge the feasibility of such work when the basic needs of communities remain unmet. Perhaps getting together the community to take social action on a critical need such as homelessness would be better supported than higher-order social changes. Techniques that work with a smaller system can also have a positive effect on groups of concerned citizens, as noted by Sliep (2005) with her work on narrative theatre, a locally adapted version of the narrative intervention we know as celebrating with a wider audience.

How do we train family therapists in South Africa? First, we need to encourage the adoption of multiple worldviews and then believe that aggressive networking will pave the way for multisystemic growth and change. The family therapy clinic at the University of KwaZulu Natal is a case in point: the staff members participate in networking by wearing many hats such as community health worker and family therapist. In one such instance, family therapy was supported by the therapist's efforts as a community empowerment officer that helped the family earn a better living through joining a self-help project in the community whilst simultaneously changing belief systems that undermined members' self-worth. Wearing both hats allowed the therapist to freely engage multisystemically and achieve goals at various systemic levels. On the training level, such cases and models are presented to students in the under- and postgraduate programs in which one of the authors is involved, underscoring the point that family therapy is not an elitist approach for middle and upper class families only (Rojano 2005).

Having a multisystemic perspective also means that we network or link with other systems that affect families. Clearly, we cannot be everything to the family. To this end, there are recorded successes of involving the clergy and accessing client spirituality for optimizing therapeutic gains (Bean et al. 2002; Joubert and Venter 2004; Kasiram et al. 2003; Neethling 2004). These authors refer to spirituality in promoting intrapsychic and interpersonal growth. Kasiram et al. (2003) point to the need to be "where the client is," for example, being aware that unconditional positive regard is often not available in the support system when most needed by HIV-positive persons. Bean et al. (2002) add that many African American people are regular church attendees and seem to seek comfort from their troubles and/or praise the Lord in gratitude through joint prayer and worship (Kasiram and Partab 2002). Perhaps these communities have fewer financial resources to celebrate achievements or mourn losses in a material fashion and therefore seek accessible communal prayer instead. It must be noted that not all families are religiously inclined and not all therapists are comfortable using spirituality; this does not mean, however, that this dimension should be excluded as a resource.

Rautenbach and Rautenbach (2004) refer to including significant others such as community members as "extended family." So pervasive is community influence in South Africa that it is enshrined in legislation governing welfare where the spirit of "ubuntu" and "ukusukuma" should guide therapists. These terms refer to having community consciousness and care as "we are who we are only because of others." This may mean using different settings for therapy to accommodate this extended family rather than the traditional clinic.

Undergraduate students at the University of KwaZulu Natal take family therapy to the homes of people where significant others such as neighbors or relatives participate in therapeutic encounters with ease. So too is the church, or a private corner in the court's grounds, a popular place for practice. These have the advantage of allowing both for the entry of others in the family system and also for a natural atmosphere within which the realities experienced by the client system may be appreciated.

Nurturance Through Nature, Arts and Drama

A land and community rich in diversity means many choices from a varying menu. In 2000, Brink took participants at his workshop on a "walk on the wild side" to demonstrate the power of using nature as nurturer to a tired spirit. He bade us picture the warmth of a fireside by the mountains, around which was told life stories. He marveled at how much people were willing to share and be open in such afresh, unrestrictive environment; he told us of how the waiting list grew since his first "walk" and how this could not pressure him into accepting "more than he could chew," as by its very nature, it needed to remain free of pollution from clutter and busy-ness. Rycroft (2004) alludes to how much is achieved when reviewing after a therapy session, almost as though it is exactly when we stop trying hard that everyone relaxes and lets true concerns surface. MacDowell (2004) discusses the value of using a wilderness experience to allow Mother Earth to guide young people that are left to manage households. The challenge of survival is used as metaphors of life through which they may review their lives and manage them more effectively. This appears to provide life lessons for the future whilst simultaneously unleashing creativity inspired by a firsthand experience of nature. All too often we are locked into and obsessed with a past that we cannot change; trails and nature walks provide metaphors for looking outside of the pain. Such experiences, encouraged by courts in restorative work with youth, are also discussed by Thulani (2004). Thus it appears that there is recognition and even support for satisfying the palate with varying menus served by nature.

Creativity derived from the arts and drama has been noted for its ability to provide fresh, culture-specific ways for renewal in the face of hopelessness. The arts have historically enabled expression in the face of despair. The authors believe that when confronted with the intensity and high levels of pain and trauma such as those associated with death to AIDS in Africa, we engage in exhaustive searches to make a difference even when these fall outside of accepted theoretical paradigms. Later, when we note their effectiveness, these searches culminate in new and indigenous theories for our context. In 1988, Lifschitz bade us develop psychotherapeutic contexts for Black families. By 2000, this bid became a resounding noise as it formed the core theme around which difference in practice was celebrated in South Africa when Rankin (2000) boldly suggested visual arts as a narrative tool in opening up possibilities for re-authoring and healing. Wakerley (2004) used both group art therapy and dance movement successfully as expressive therapies in her work with AIDS orphans and rape survivors in Alexandra and Mamelodi, South Africa. Sometimes language is too confining to relate the problem-saturated story. So, individually oriented therapies provide a platform to initiate group and community-oriented interventions.

In this vein, Naidoo (2004) refers to the value of group acting and narration to educate an audience. Richter et al. (2004) mention the value of multimedia channels for influencing attitudes and behavior such as on male domination in non-use of the condom. Sliep (2005) uses another form of communication with "more than one," that is, narrative theatre, to hear stories of shame and horror amongst disempowered women who have had terrible injustices inflicted on them. United in this fashion, they may gain courage and strength.

Conclusion

Community as context cannot be ignored in South Africa or any other part of the world. This paper explored the many wonderful ideas and practices by therapists who wish to meaningfully exchange with their clients at individual, group, and/or community levels. Although these innovators demonstrate unusual ideas in breaking away from the pack, they couch changes and adjustments in traditional family therapy language. We believe that we have evolved from merely thinking about the need for indigenizing to actually practicing differently. We have a wealth of changes to show off as we comfortably embrace community, culture, and difference into family-oriented work. We should actively collaborate to strengthen and publish our work for a local and international market that is increasingly working with families and communities that do not fit the traditional, dominant mold. Let us set forth on this journey with energy and enthusiasm, knowing that practices today may last but a season, until change and evolution take us into the possibilities of the future.

References

Ajila, C. O. (2004). Hope fostering among the Yoruba-speaking people of Nigeria: The use of proverbs, cognomen, prayers and names. *Anthropologist, 6*, 141–146.

Akinyela, M. M.. (2004, May). *Meeting the trickster at the crossroads: Oral cultures and the use of metaphor as a resource in therapeutic conversations*. Paper presented at the 9th SAAMFT International Conference, Durban, South Africa.

Barnard, F. (2004, May). *Developing and evaluating a parenting programme to facilitate informed decision-making about high-risk behaviour in adolescence*. Paper presented at the 9th SAA-MFT International Conference, Durban, South Africa.

Bean, R. A., Benjamin, J. P., & Bedell, T. M. (2002). Developing culturally competent marriage and family therapists: Treatment guidelines for non-American therapists working with African-American families. *Journal of Marital and Family Therapy, 28,* 153–164.

Brink, J. (2000, April). *Take a walk on the wild side.* Workshop presented at the 8th International Conference of SAAMFT, Cape Town, South Africa.

Hall, N. (2000). Postmodern therapy in the Zimbabwean context: How good a fit? In S. Shuda, R. Mauer, A. R. Haarhoff, & D. Haarhoff (Eds.), *One nation: Many families. Gender, hope and training: Papers from the 8th International Conference of SAAMFT* (pp. 87–96). Cape Town, South Africa: Creda Communications.

Hernandez, P., Almeida, R., & Dolan-Del Vecchio, K. (2005). Critical consciousness, accountability and empowerment: Key processes for helping families heal. *Family Process, 44,* 105–120.

Jeewa, A. (2005). *Substance abuse in the 21st century: An empowerment model.* Unpublished master's thesis, University of KwaZulu Natal, Durban, South Africa.

Joubert, N., & Venter, C. (2004, May). *The development and evaluation of a biblically-based therapy programme for a congregation.* Paper presented at the 9th SAAMFT International Conference, Durban, South Africa.

Kasiram, M. (2000). Living in hope: Therapy for the disadvantaged. In S. Shuda, R. Mauer, A. R. Haarhoff, & D. Haarhoff (Eds.), *One nation: Many families. Gender, hope and training: Papers from the 8th International Conference of SAAMFT* (pp. 102–111). Cape Town, South Africa: Creda Communications.

Kasiram, M., & Partab, P. (2002). Facilitating grieving through culture and community: A South African perspective. *Maatskaplike Werk/Social Work, 38*(1), 39–44.

Kasiram, M., Partab, R., Dano, B., & van Greunnen, J. (2003). Managing HIV/AIDS: *Guidelines for counsellors, caregivers and faith-based practitioners*. Durban, South Africa, Print Connection.

Lee, M. Y., & Mjelde-Mossey, L. (2004). Cultural dissonance among generations: A solution-focused approach with East Asian elders and their families. *Journal of Marital and Family Therapy, 30,* 497–513.

Lifschitz, S. (1988). The story of the cave or finding ways to create psychotherapeutic contexts for black clients. In J. Mason & J. Rubenstein (Eds.), *Family therapy in South Africa today* (pp. 46–51). Pinetown, Durban, South Africa: Robprint.

MacDowell, M. (2004). The Spirit of wilderness: The benefits of a wilderness trail for child-headed families. Paper presentation at the 9th SAAMFT International Conference, Durban, South Africa.

McDowell, T., Fang, S. R., Brownlee, K., Young, C. G., & Khanna, A. (2002). Transforming an MFT Program: A model for enhancing diversity. *Journal of Marital and Family Therapy, 28,* 179–191.

McNamee, S. (2004). Promiscuity in the practice of family therapy. *Journal of Family Therapy, 26,* 224–244.

Morkel, E. (2004, May). *Therapy with children affected by divorce*. Paper presented at the 9th SAAMFT International Conference, Durban, South Africa.

Naidoo, P. (2004). *An investigation into the factors contributing to unplanned pregnancy at the University of KwaZulu Natal, Westville Campus*. Unpublished Master's thesis, University of KwaZulu Natal, Durban, South Africa.

Naidoo, S., & Kasiram, M. (2003). Social work in South Africa: Quo Vadis? *Maatskaplike Werk/ Social Work, 39*(4), 372–380.

Nair, Y. (2004, May). *Information, self-empowerment or collective action? Working with youth to prevent HI V/A IDS.* Paper presented at the 9th SAAMFT International Conference, Durban, South Africa.

Neethling, I. (2004, May). *The soul of healing: Uncovering the spiritual dimension in therapy.* Paper presented at the 9th SAAMFT International Conference, Durban, South Africa.

Nell, V., & Seedat, M. (1988). "Western-style" family therapy in the Soweto primary healthcare system. In J. B. Mason & J. Rubenstein (Eds.), *Family therapy in South Africa today* (pp. 40–45). Pinetown, Durban, South Africa: Robprint.

Oliphant, E. (2005). *Challenges to family therapy in South Africa.* Unpublished manuscript.

Petty, A. (2004, May). *A developmental approach to reaching traumatized children in kinship care placements in the Umlazi area.* Paper presented at the 9th SAAMFT International Conference, Durban, South Africa.

Rankin, J. (2000). Drawing rich descriptions: Telling stories through the visual arts. In R. Shuda, R. Mauer, A. R. Haarhoff, & D. Haarhoff (Eds.), *One nation: Many families. Gender, hope and training: Papers from the 8th International Conference of SAAMFT* (pp. 121–130). Cape Town, South Africa: Creda Communications.

Rautenbach, M. P., & Rautenbach, E. (2004). Sustaining community growth: A familial perspective from the northern cape. Paper presentation at the 9th SAAMFT International Conference, Durban, South Africa.

Richter, L., Dawes, A., & Manegold, J. (2004, May). *Promoting men's care and protection of children through multimedia channels.* Paper presented at the 9th SAAMFT International Conference, Durban, South Africa.

Rojano, R. (2005). The practice of community family therapy. *Family Process, 43*(1), 59–78.

Rundell, F. (2000). Co-vision: An alternate to supervision. In S. Shuda, R. Mauer, A. R. Haarhoff, & D. Haarhoff (Eds.), *One nation: Many families. Gender, hope and training: Papers from the 8th International Conference of SAAMFT* (pp. 143–151). Cape Town, South Africa: Creda Communications.

Rycroft, P. (2004). When theory abandons us: Wading through the swampy lowlands of practice. *Journal of Family Therapy, 26,* 245–259.

Sliep, Y. (2000, April). *Interviewing HIV/AIDS affected women.* Workshop and interview at the 8th International SAAMFT Conference. Cape Town, South Africa.

Sliep, Y. (2005). *Innovative techniques: Narrative theatre in working with abuse.* Durban, South Africa. Unpublished manuscript.

Thulani, Z. (2004, May). *Wilderness diversions.* Paper presented at the 9th SAAMFT International Conference, Durban, South Africa.

Wakerley, A. (2004, May). *The use of art and dance-movement therapies in an African context.* Paper presented at the 9th SAAMFT International Conference, Durban, South Africa.

Winfield, J., and students of the Department of Child and Youth Development, DIT. (2004, May). *Restorative conferencing: Indigenous philosophy in contemporary practice with young people and families.* Paper presented at the 9th SAAMFT International Conference, Durban, South Africa.

Nuestra Casa [Our Home]: From the Family to the Community

Beatriz Molina†, Ćielo de Cure, Carmen Maria de Salazar, Katia de Rosales, Silvia de Navarro, Maria Teresa de Sabbagh, Maria de Theran and Daisy Barros

The creation of Nuestra Casa [Our Home] Family Care Center arose from our interdisciplinary group's research and clinical work with the families attending Hogar CREA (Center for the Re-education of Addicts), a therapeutic residential community for the treatment of addictions in Barranquilla, Colombia. Hogar CREA is an international movement that started in Puerto Rico in 1966. In 1984, when the movement was brought to us in Colombia, it sparked a very positive community reaction. Substance abuse had been on the rise, and many wanted to help. Our group of mental health professionals began exploring ways to increase our family consultation skills while addressing the problems experienced by families of Barranquilla and surrounding towns.

Ramón Rojano, a Colombian psychiatrist, introduced family therapy to our team in 1985, which became the basis for all our work. For the next 19 years, the family therapy team continued to meet on its own, bringing in trained family therapists from Argentina and other places, improving our expertise in family work. During the last decade[1], our team also forged an alliance with the larger family therapy community in the city of Medellin, a practitioner community that pioneered the development of family therapy in Colombia beginning in the late 1970s. Thus, provided with ongoing training seminars, consultation and individual supervision, we began to envision creating a nongovernmental organization dedicated exclusively to provide family services.

Editors' note: First published in 2005, American Family Therapy Academy Monograph Series.

Sadly, Beatriz Molina passed away before this volume was instituted. Her co-authors dedicate this chapter to her.

---

[1] Editors' note: previous to 2005, the first publication of this chapter.

C. M. de Salazar (✉) · K. de Rosales · Ć. de Cure · S. de Navarro · M. T. de Sabbagh · M. de Theran · D. Barros
Fundación Nuestra Casa (Our Home), Barranquilla, Colombia
e-mail: carmenmaria_g@yahoo.com

B. Molina†
Universidad Pontificia Bolivariana, Medellin, Colombia

T. Nelson, H. Winawer (eds.), *Critical Topics in Family Therapy*,
AFTA SpringerBriefs in Family Therapy, DOI 10.1007/978-3-319-03248-1_8,

Nuestra Casa Foundation became a reality in 1997, when it began officially to deliver services. Nuestra Casa's mission is stated as follows: "to work towards the development and strengthening of families through preventive, educational, therapeutic, and legal programs serving families with a community approach?" Today, the agency operates out of its own "home" a large house with rooms for various types of group activities and several individual counseling offices. It has its own administrative staff and a multidisciplinary clinical staff of social workers, psychologists, family therapists, educators, and attorneys. Almost all of us work part-time, partly on a fee-for-service basis and partly *pro bono.* Service contracts, educational seminars, direct fees from clients, and donations financially support the center. Services are provided at low or no cost, thus opening the doors to many who could not afford counseling fees from private practitioners. Administratively, Nuestra Casa has an infrastructure that flows through a Board of Directors and Founders Committee, into working teams feeding into a program coordinator level.

Services are provided not only to individuals and families, but also to schools, educational institutions, businesses, and the community at large. Nuestra Casa addresses a great variety of issues, including intrafamily violence and addiction, stressful family life cycle transitions, family disintegration, separation, conflicts and breakups, and other types of relational and emotional problems. The primary goal is to strengthen families, providing them with tools to enhance communication and cohesiveness. Additionally, families are trained to identify for themselves specific situations that require therapeutic intervention. The following interventions are offered:

- Preventive educational services provided through seminars, workshops, forums, and conferences.
- A special "couples' school" that offers education and ongoing support.
- Individual therapy for adults, adolescents, and children.
- Traditional systemic and postmodern family and couples therapy.
- Legal family counseling including educational, preventive, and mediation services.

These activities were shaped taking into account cultural differences in our communities, always allowing for inclusion and contribution from various client groups. Educational workshops tailored to specific constituencies also proved to be an effective type of community action. In seeking to attain greater impact, the Center decided to include some family therapy concepts in educational presentations. Great emphasis has also been put on fostering the integration and development of Nuestra Casa's team, which operates as its own family. Important activities include Group Integration, Bingo, and the Christmas Novena and Skirts Party, a traditional celebration from the Caribbean coast of Colombia. Many internal celebrations help to increase our group's cohesiveness, such as birthdays, Mother's Day, and the Center's anniversary. We also make time for spiritual activities, including the celebration of religious holidays and retreats. The spirit of our team shows clearly when we sing our own original hymn, "Prayer for the Family." In addition, we have worked to make our interventions more culturally competent by adapting them to the paradigm of the Colombian coastal community—los Costeños—within the Colombian cultural mosaic. Evaluation and inclusion of the extended family allows staff and family to harness the solidarity of relatives and friends and the tendency to practical problem-solving, which is inherent to Costeño culture.

Nuestra Casa's success has been built on several specific strategies. These include dedicating significant time to building and enriching a powerful multidisciplinary team; developing strong inter-institutional agreements; maintaining working partnerships with businesses, public, and private institutions; maintaining strong linkages with the community; and building a very strong volunteer workforce. We have contracts with the Instituto Colombiano de Bienestar Familiar (Colombian Family Welfare Institute) and the United Nations Preventive Project for Strengthening of the Family. Institutional and community bonds are strong enough now to support a large roster of clinical activities, and draw a significant number of attendees. For its conferences and forums, the agency is able to mobilize large numbers of individuals at a time, ranging from 100 to 700 participants.

Throughout the years, Nuestra Casa has wrestled with several challenges; maintaining financial viability has been a constant issue. Poor socioeconomic conditions make it difficult for our clients to afford even the reduced fees that we charge per session. Traditional beliefs and prejudices create skepticism in some families, constraining them from pursuing personal and family transformation through counseling or participation. The community as a whole is not sufficiently familiar with the concept of seeking professional help for family problems. To achieve better visibility and strengthen our economic support base, Nuestra Casa still has a lot of work to do in public relations and marketing. Use of the media for community education campaigns is not yet at the level we would desire. Although Nuestra Casa was created to serve all socioeconomic groups, the poorest families still do not benefit sufficiently. The team is seeking more resources to enable us to add services, for example, a satellite office in one of the very financially deprived neighborhoods of Barranquilla. Because our program is managed with a very lean administrative infrastructure, it is difficult at times to effectively manage our inter-institutional contracts. Finally, a research division we envisioned has not yet been organized.

We have been asked, "If you could start over again, what would you do differently?" Based on what we have learned through our experience thus far and on our ultimate goals, we would have preferred a location with easier access to low-income families. We also would have preferred to engage in a more consolidated search for national and international funding to subsidize our work with families who lack resources. Over time, many adjustments and improvements were made both at the operational and programmatic levels. To make our services more flexible and available to individuals and families, Nuestra Casa extended its hours of operation and increased the number of therapists.

Our therapeutic model benefited from refinements included later: cotherapy, reflective teams, and solution-focused interventions. A family therapist runs the risk of establishing a vertical relationship with clients and using the power given to him/her to define and dominate needs and solutions. One of the crucial contributions of family therapy to our institution has been the move toward a bidirectional and cooperative relationship with client families. As Harlene Anderson (1997) explains, the therapist, the person, and the family are equal partners in the conversation; the first is an expert in understandings and possibilities, and the second is an expert on himself and the situation. Therapists should adapt themselves to families, not the opposite. Inter-institutional work should be broadened to examination of policies, practices, and financing that affect family welfare. Difficulties in life are best understood through a systemic lens, which gives participants a sense of responsibility for their own destiny. Michael White has commented that this way of working is also a source of support and inspiration for the therapist. We have found that working in community is an antidote for professional fatigue.

After many years of intensive training, teamwork, and community practice, we at Nuestra Casa have learned important lessons. The most valuable have been to think and treat the family as a system in its structure and language, to believe in the family's potential to change, to empower consultation through listening to and privileging a client's needs, and to empower families by seeing them as authors of their own change. Nuestra Casa planted the seed of systemic family therapy as the basis of the mission, watered it with community work, fertilized it through links with social institutions, and energized it through the team's commitment to collaboration. Out of this project, two principles have emerged: appreciation of the relational world in which we live, and a deeper understanding that personal difficulties are best resolved through a network that connects the individual, the family, and the community.

References

Anderson, H. (1997). *Conversation, language, and possibilities.* New York, NY: Basic Books.

Part III

Systemic Responses to Disaster: Stories of the Aftermath of Hurricane Katrina, 2007

—John Sargent, Guest Editor

Helping Children Heal After the Hurricanes: An Innovative Training Approach

Katherine T. Volk, Kristina Konnath and Ellen L. Bassuk

> We saw 2,000 people that first night in the Astrodome. Some had no shoes on their feet. They'd seen bodies floating. The children had experienced all of this just as the adults had. Children's mental health is not on people's radar screens. How will these experiences affect them as adults?

A staff member from Health Care for the Homeless of Harrison County, Texas, which set up emergent healthcare in the Astrodome as hurricane evacuees started to arrive.

When Hurricanes Katrina and Rita hit the Gulf Coast, their punch lasted far longer than the initial event. Biloxi and Gulfport witnessed a storm surge of 20 to 30 feet. Most of New Orleans and the surrounding parishes were plunged underwater, destroying entire communities. Neighborhoods that were home to generations of families were left in rubble. The media described families rescued from rooftops, families separated from one another, and families living in the Superdome, Astrodome, and even on the Interstate (Boo 2005; CNN 2006; Horne 2006; Kalb and Murr 2005).

Families and children were separated for weeks, even months. Some remain apart even today.

These communities were not strangers to destruction and loss. Many families displaced by the hurricanes had experienced other losses in their lives, as well as various unpredictable stresses associated with living in severe poverty. For them, the storms' destruction came on top of other unresolved difficulties, frequently leading to complex emotional responses. In the weeks and months after the storms, it became increasingly clear that for many families, the impact of cumulative traumatic stresses would have long-lasting mental health consequences. The National

Editors' note: First published in 2007, American Family Therapy Academy Monograph Series.

K. T. Volk (✉) · E. L. Bassuk
Center of Social Innovation, Needham MA, USA
e-mail: kvolk@center4si.com

K. Konnath
Justice Resource Institute (JRI), Boston MA, USA

T. Nelson, H. Winawer (eds.), *Critical Topics in Family Therapy*,
AFTA SpringerBriefs in Family Therapy, DOI 10.1007/978-3-319-03248-1_9,

Table 1 Key Child Indicators in the Gulf States

State	Infant mortality ranking[a]	Food insecurity (%)[b]	Community violence: A child or teen is killed by gunfire…[c]	% of fourth graders reading below grade level[d]	% of children living in poverty[e]
Alabama	47	12.2	every 5 days	78	23.6
Florida	29	10.8	every 3 days	68	18.6
Louisiana	48	11.8	every 3 days	80	27.5
Mississippi	49	15.8	every 6 days	82	28.8
Texas	13	16.4	every day	73	21.8

[a] Source: US Department of Health and Human Services, National Center for Health Statistics (2003)

[b] Food insecurity is a condition of uncertain availability of or ability to acquire safe, nutritious food in socially acceptable ways. Source: Bread for the World Institute 2006

[c] Source: Children's Defense Fund 2004

[d] Source: US Department of Education, National Assessment of Educational Progress (2003)

[e] Source: Table P114, US Department of Commerce, Bureau of the Census 2002

Center on Family Homelessness (The National Center; http://www.familyhomelessness.org/) shaped its response with this understanding.

The National Center has spent the past year [2006] working with service providers in the hurricane-impacted regions of the Gulf Coast. This article describes life in the Gulf States before and after the hurricanes, particularly as it relates to children's well-being and mental health status. It then reviews The National Center's efforts to train service providers to understand the impact of traumatic stress on children and their caregivers. The article concludes with a discussion of future plans.

Life in the Gulf States Before the Hurricanes

The Gulf States—Alabama, Louisiana, Florida, Texas, and Mississippi—often finish last on a variety of child indicators when compared to other U.S. states. For example, in 1999, The National Center ranked each state according to children's risk for homelessness (the higher the ranking, the greater the risk). Louisiana had the highest ranking of the 50 states. Mississippi earned a ranking of 45, Alabama 43, and Texas 36 (Bassuk 1999). These ratings and more recent data indicate that severe poverty and its associated ills have exacted a high toll. Many families are extremely poor, and lack decent affordable housing, medical care, and adequate health services. Not surprisingly, the ravages of poverty lead to compromised outcomes among the children. Table 1 highlights the precarious situation of many Gulf Coast children.

High poverty rates, community violence, hunger, and educational challenges characterize many children's experiences. However, despite the challenges of poverty and violence, strong family ties exist in many neighborhoods, particularly in New Orleans. Journalist Jed Horne, who won a Pulitzer Prize for his role in *The*

Times-Picayune's coverage of Hurricane Katrina, describes New Orleans as a city of "insular self-contentment" in which many residents "in a long lifetime…had never left for much more than a weekend away" (Horne 2006, p. 26). The National Center's interviews with community members reaffirm this sentiment, describing neighborhoods in which families often stayed for generations, forming close-knit communities that provided strong social supports and sustenance for its members.

After the Hurricanes

In February, 2006, Operation Assist, a collaborative effort of the Children's Health Fund and the National Center for Disaster Preparedness at the Columbia University Mailman School of Public Health, surveyed 1,000 Louisiana residents living in FEMA-subsidized community settings (e.g., trailer parks and hotels). Researchers concluded that

> The medical and mental health needs documented in this report may be regarded as the consequence of inadequately treated chronic diseases, psychological and emotional traumas secondary to the chaos and despair of a massive dislocation, and the social deprivations of the chronically poor and the newly impoverished. At a deeper level, though, the problems relate to the loss of stability in people's lives: families that are increasingly fragile, children who are disengaged from schools, and the wholesale loss of community, workplace, and health care providers and institutions. (Abramson and Garfield 2006, p. 1)

The Abramson and Garfield study quantified the powerful impact of the 2005 hurricane season on children's health. The authors reported the following:

- 34% of children had at least one diagnosed chronic medical condition, a rate one-third higher than the general U.S. pediatric population. Displaced children were more likely to suffer from asthma, behavioral or conduct problems, developmental delays or physical impairments, and learning disabilities when compared with children surveyed in urban Louisiana areas in 2003.
- Nearly 50% of parents reported that at least one child in their household had emotional or behavioral difficulties that were not present prior to the hurricane such as feeling sad or depressed, being nervous or afraid, or having problems sleeping or getting along with others.
- Parents whose families had been displaced were more likely to report that their children's health was fair or poor, a rate more than three times as high as the U.S. general pediatric population.

Just as the children in the study demonstrated health difficulties, so did their parents. Using a standardized mental health screening tool that measures the extent to which poor mental health interferes with daily activities, researchers learned that parents and mothers in particular, scored poorly:

- More than half of the women caregivers scored at levels consistent with those who had clinically-diagnosed psychiatric problems such as depression or anxiety disorders.

- Children whose parents scored very low on this assessment were two and a half times as likely to have experienced emotional or behavioral problems after the hurricane.

Researchers also found that caregivers felt more overwhelmed and less safe:

- Female caregivers were six times as likely to report that they were not coping well with the daily demands of parenting when compared to parents in a pre-Katrina survey of urban Louisianans.
- Almost half of parents and other caregivers believed that their children were either never or only sometimes safe in their communities compared to 21 % of caregivers answering the same question in urban Louisiana pre-Katrina.

These statistics are both alarming and unsurprising. As these fragile families patched together the pieces of their lives, organizations and average Americans struggled to respond to the catastrophe. For some, it meant turning their elementary schools into de facto community centers, providing safe havens for children and families alike. Others opened up their homes to evacuees or converted their churches into make-shift shelters. Community agencies already working with vulnerable populations began the arduous task of long-term recovery by offering counseling, healthcare, and other vital human services to deal with evacuees' complex needs. Among these agencies, family shelter providers and others who worked with those experiencing homelessness realized that a new subset of Americans now knew what it was like to live without a home.

The National Center's Response

The National Center was uniquely positioned to respond to the aftermath of Hurricanes Katrina and Rita. Founded in 1988, The National Center had spent many years working with families and others experiencing homelessness. We understand that losing a home frequently results in a loss of security, reassuring routines, a sense of having a place in the world, and ties to religious communities, schools, neighbors, and friends. Because the experience of losing a home is frequently overwhelming, sudden, and catastrophic, it can be viewed as a traumatic stress. As Judith Herman (1992) has eloquently described, traumatic events call into question

> …the system of attachments and meaning that link individual to community. They undermine the belief systems that give meaning to human experience. They violate the victim's faith in a natural or divine order and cast the victim into a state of existential crisis. (p. 51)

Drawing on this knowledge, The National Center created the Katrina Project, a long-term effort to train service providers in the Gulf region to help families heal from traumatic stress. Trainings focused specifically and intentionally on children, their caregivers, and the relationship between them. Participants were provided with practical resources, including the PEACH curriculum (Physical and Emotional Awareness for Children Who Are Homeless; Volk et al. 2006), a physical and emotional awareness program for young children without homes.

The Katrina Project aimed to train "second responders," those who work with children and families every day. These second responders include teachers, principals, social workers, counselors, case managers, child care workers, shelter providers, healthcare providers, and other caregivers. To date, more than 500 caregivers from 65 communities in Arkansas, Florida, Louisiana, Mississippi, and Texas have attended the trainings, which were offered to communities free of charge, thanks to the generous support of the W. K. Kellogg Foundation. Trainings have also been sponsored by SAMHSA's National Resource and Training Center on Homelessness and Mental Illness and the National Child Traumatic Stress Network.

To conduct these trainings, The National Center partnered with two key national organizations: OrganWise Guys, Inc. and the National Health Care for the Homeless Council (The Council). OrganWise Guys, Inc., a wellness curriculum company based in Atlanta, GA, was able to draw on already-strong relationships with university extension agents through Mississippi State University, Louisiana State University, and the University of Arkansas to bring this training to principals, teachers, nurses, coaches, social workers, and others.

The Council is a twenty-year-old organization of local health agencies, individual clinicians, respite care providers, and people who have experienced homelessness. The Council and its Health Care for the Homeless (HCH) grantees represent the nation's leading healthcare provider for homeless individuals, families, children, and youth in more than 140 communities across the country. HCH staff helped to set up healthcare systems for hurricane evacuees in the Astrodome and provided emergency care to thousands in the days following Katrina. As The National Center planned trainings for organizations serving families experiencing homelessness (either due to "traditional" reasons or to circumstances related to the hurricane evacuation), The Council proved instrumental in facilitating relationships with local coalitions for the homeless and other similar organizations. It also provided training content in self-care, grief, and loss based on *Shelter Health: Essentials of Care for People Living in Shelter* (Kraybill and Olivet 2006). This guide was developed by The Council in the wake of the hurricanes to assist those who set up shelters for people displaced by the hurricanes and those who operated pre-existing shelters that absorbed evacuees from the storms.

Training Content

The Katrina Project trainings helped providers understand the nature of traumatic stress and its long-term impact. Specifically, the training content was divided into five segments:

1. Defining traumatic stress and the human stress response
2. Assessing clients
3. Promoting healing
4. Using practical tools: the PEACH curriculum
5. Addressing self-care, grief, and loss

By the end of the training, participants were able to connect what they learned about the range of responses to traumatic stress with the behaviors they had observed in children and families. They also received practical tools to use in their daily work life and were given the opportunity to reflect on their own experiences as caregivers working amidst profound grief and loss. In the next few pages, we discuss each of the five components of the training in greater detail.

Defining Traumatic Stress and the Human Stress Response. In the words of Judith Herman (1992), "Traumatic events overwhelm the ordinary systems of care that give people a sense of control, connection, and meaning" (p. 33). A traumatic event is sudden and unexpected, and perceived as dangerous. It may involve a threat of physical harm or actual physical harm, leading to intense fear, and overwhelms one's immediate ability to cope. Traumatic experiences may include the unexpected loss of a loved one, physical or sexual abuse, community violence, terrorism, natural disasters, and more. Most people experience at least one traumatic event over the course of their lives.

In the Katrina Project, we began the trainings by describing the human stress response: "fight-flight-freeze." We asked participants to imagine themselves driving on the highway when a car swerves into their lane and veers away, barely missing their vehicle. Their imagined responses to this event—nervous, tense, frozen, jittery—mirror the human stress response. These responses are generally short-lived and most people return to their usual level of functioning after the event.

We then asked participants to imagine that every time they got into their car, they got into an accident or near accident. Many imagined that they would stop driving, stay home, and avoid places where accidents had occurred. As traumatic experiences layer on top of one another, the brain responds accordingly. We explained that often people see, hear, or feel things that remind them of dangers that have happened in the past, which are called triggers. The brain learns to recognize these reminders because in the past it was important to respond quickly; it then begins to associate danger with these triggers. In the aftermath of the hurricanes, the repeated newscasts of the tragedy, multiple transitions, and even rainy days were often triggers for those who survived. Especially on rainy days, children often responded with hyperactivity, unfocused energy, and difficulty responding to directions. Participants learned that children who have experienced traumatic stressors may be derailed from their normal developmental trajectory, no longer achieving usual developmental milestones. They may also show regressive behaviors such as bedwetting, and behavior that is inappropriate for their ages.

Assessing Clients. We encouraged training participants to consider five factors in assessing the impact of traumatic stress on families: the characteristics of the traumatic event(s), the family's current and past history, the age and developmental status of the children, caregiver responses, and attachment relationships (Kinninburgh and Blaustein 2005). Although Hurricanes Katrina and Rita were one-time events, they inflicted multiple traumas that will have long-term consequences for many Americans. Our trainings encouraged participants to look at "the whole picture," especially the impact of prior traumatic events. How did the child fare in school prior to the storms? What was the family's experience of the hurricane? What is the family's current living situation? The more participants understand about the families with whom they work, the better they will be able to respond in a way that is sensitive to the complex traumas families have experienced.

Promoting Healing. Trainees discussed concrete ways to help children heal. This section of the training focused primarily on safety. What are ways that children and families can be made to feel emotionally and physically safe? Through simple strategies such as relaxation exercises, children learn that they can have some control over their bodies, which in turn helps them regulate their emotions and restores a sense of safety. More complex strategies, such as creating routine and predictability—even amidst chaotic circumstances—are also essential to helping children heal. We encouraged caregivers working in classroom settings to establish and maintain routines and to give children ample warning if routines were to change. We encouraged shelter workers to apply these principles to their settings as well.

Using Practical Tools: The PEACH Curriculum. One of the core principles of the Katrina Project trainings was to ensure that participants were given concrete resources to bring back to their communities. The PEACH curriculum is an innovative way to operationalize many of the concepts taught in the training. PEACH is a concrete way for children to make the connection between the ways their bodies react to traumatic stress and the emotions that they are experiencing. This linkage helps them learn to regulate and better express their feelings.

The PEACH curriculum consists of a specially-tailored set of materials (e.g., books, videos, and games) that address the unique circumstances of children who have experienced the traumatic stress of losing their homes. Divided into 13 one-hour sessions, the program begins by helping children understand how their bodies function (Physical; e.g., their hearts pump blood, their lungs need fresh air, etc.) and then introduces emotional health concepts as a way to help children understand how their bodies react to traumatic stress.

Training attendees received instructions on how to implement PEACH in their setting and received all of the curriculum materials at no charge. Attendees also had the opportunity to apply for small grants to help them implement PEACH in their community.

Addressing Self-Care, Grief, and Loss. A portion of each training focused on self-care. Providers expressed their appreciation for this focus, particularly at a time when many felt overwhelmed and depleted by the relentless demands of recovery work. Many providers were hurricane evacuees themselves and had been living in temporary FEMA trailers and other transitional arrangements. As part of self-care training, we spent time discussing the tremendous grief and loss that service providers witness as they work with clients who have lost so much. Through thoughtful discussion, reflection, and occasional humor, trainers and participants alike spent time discussing ways to find renewal and resiliency in their work.

Community Feedback and Future Plans

Service providers have a strong desire to learn about how traumatic stress impacts the children with whom they work, and their responses to the trainings were overwhelmingly positive. They were grateful for the additional knowledge, skills, and support, and the materials they could take back to their organizations. Training participants have repeatedly contacted us, asking for additional materials and information. Most important, they felt the trainings addressed their own needs for self-care. The National Center will pursue strategies that help service providers and the families with whom they work over the short and long term. Our short-term approach is to continue with our partners to offer trainings to service providers on traumatic stress and its implications for children and families. Given the resounding response from community leaders as well as the continuing needs of teachers, providers, parents, and community members, we plan to broaden the content of the curriculum and add support materials, as well as expand our target training population to a wider geographic area and additional professional sectors.

We believe that the most effective training occurs when the information is experiential, interactive, continuous, and closely targeted to the needs of the providers and the children. Thus, our long-term strategy involves working in-depth with selected communities. Ideally, a major goal would be to increase local capacity to respond to posttraumatic stress in children by offering a train-the-trainer approach, in which a cadre of local providers become "experts" and are then able to provide ongoing training to other local personnel. The children and families impacted by Hurricanes Katrina and Rita have endured countless traumas. Service providers have felt overwhelmed at the daunting effects these traumas have had on the children they care about so deeply. The Katrina Project has given training participants and their colleagues a framework to understand children's experiences, tools to help them heal, and support to continue with their important work.

References

Abramson, D., & Garfield, R. N. (2006). *On the edge: Children and families displaced by Hurricanes Katrina and Rita face a looming medical and mental health crisis*. New York, NY: Columbia University Mailman School of Public Health National Center for Disaster Preparedness.

Bassuk, E. (1999). *Homeless children: America's new outcasts*. Newton Centre, MA: The National Center on Family Homelessness.

Boo, K. (2005, November 28). Shelter and the storm. *New Yorker,* 82–97.

Bread for the World Institute. (2006). *Frontline issues in nutrition assistance*: *Hunger report*. Washington, DC: Author.

Children's Defense Fund. (2004). *Children in the states*. Washington, DC: Children's defense fund. Retrieved December, 2006, from http://www.childrensdefense.org/site/PageServer?pagename=research_state_information_children_in_the_states

CNN. (2006, April 25). *Depression, anxiety in Katrina's kids: Patterns of hurricane's psychological effects emerging*. Retrieved December, 2006, from http://www.cnn.com

Herman, J. (1992). *Trauma and recovery*. New York, NY: Basic Books.

Horne, J. (2006). *Breach of faith: Hurricane Katrina and the near death of a great American city*. New York, NY: Random House.

Kalb, C., & Murr, A. (2005, December 12). The cost of the Katrina effect. *Newsweek*, 66–70.

Kinninburgh, K., & Blaustein, M. (2005). *Attachment, self-regulation, and competency: A comprehensive framework for intervention with complexly traumatized youth*. Brookline, MA: The Trauma Center.

Kraybill, K., & Olivet, J. (2006). *Shelter health: Essentials of care for people living in shelter*. Nashville, TN: National Health Care for the Homeless Council.

U.S. Department of Commerce, Bureau of the Census. (2002). *American community survey*. Retrieved December, 2006, from the American FactFinder website, http://www.census.gov

U.S. Department of Education, National Assessment of Educational Progress. (2003). *The nation's report card: Reading highlights 2003, Table 3.*

U.S. Department of Health and Human Services, National Center for Health Statistics. (2003, September 18). Deaths: Final data for 2001. *National Vital Statistics Report, 52*(3), Table 33.

Volk, K., Bassuk, E., & Foster, S. (2006). *Physical and emotional awareness for children who are homeless: A tool kit for transitional settings*. Newton Centre, MA: National Center on Family Homelessness.

Part IV

Neuroscience and Family Therapy: Integrations and Applications, 2008
—Martha Edwards, Guest Editor

“News from Neuroscience”: Applications to Couple Therapy

Mona DeKoven Fishbane

Consider the following scenario: A couple comes to a therapist, and, in presenting their complaints, the partners escalate so quickly that the therapist is left breathless and sidelined. Much of the literature in couple therapy focuses on how to empower both couple and therapist to translate and transform this gut-wrenching wild ride into a manageable process that can ultimately lead to greater calm, safety, and generosity within the couple. In recent years, findings from neuroscience have shed light on the workings of our emotional brain, and on the interplay between minds in intimate relationships. In this essay I will discuss how I integrate “interpersonal neurobiology” (Siegel 1999) in my own work as a couple therapist (see also Fishbane 2007).

In my practice, I utilize “news from neuroscience” in several ways. For one, learning about the brain can deepen our theories of human development, relationships, and therapy. The fundamental questions of what it means to be a human being, what we share with and how we differ from other mammals, how we end up on the “low road” of reactivity and how we can regain the “high road” of thoughtfulness and self-regulation—questions so central to therapy—are all addressed by neuroscience. Much of our relational/systemic theory in family therapy is validated by interpersonal neurobiology and its emphasis on how our social/emotional brains link up with each other. Second, findings from neurobiology help shape specific interventions I use in couple therapy. Finally, I incorporate neurobiology psychoeducationally—or “neuroeducationally”—with couples, empowering them to understand and modulate their own reactions and behavior. I will explore these various influences of interpersonal neurobiology on my work as a couple therapist.

Neuroscience research makes it clear that, as humans, we are born to connect with others, and that it is through our connection with others that our brains get wired (Goleman 2006; Siegel and Hartzell 2003). Critical aspects of the development of

Editors’ note: First published in 2008, American Family Therapy Academy Monograph Series.

M. D. Fishbane (✉)
Chicago, IL, USA
e-mail: mfishba@aol.com

T. Nelson, H. Winawer (eds.), *Critical Topics in Family Therapy*,
AFTA SpringerBriefs in Family Therapy, DOI 10.1007/978-3-319-03248-1_10,

the young child's brain depend on attunement and attachment between child and parents or caregivers (Schore 2003; Siegel and Hartzell 2003). In the interplay of genetics and experience, nature and nurture, our brains develop neuronal connections that underlie thought, emotion, and behavior. Our affective life is particularly influenced by our early environment because the right hemisphere functioning from birth—responsible for much of our emotional life—is most impacted by parental attunement or lack thereof. The left hemisphere, responsible for language and logic, develops later. Likewise, explicit memory is not available in the first years of life; implicit, preverbal memory registers our early life experiences, and this influences current reactions even though we may not be able to recall explicitly what has triggered our feelings.

As adults, we carry these implicit emotional memories into our current interpersonal interactions; they are particularly potent in our most intimate relationships. When partners become reactive with each other, one or both may be experiencing a triggering of old emotional memories. The flavor of these memories often makes the current escalation seem irrational; the client may not have words to put to his or her experience, may not explicitly recall a past trauma, and may try to justify an emotional reaction on the basis of current couple issues. In my experience, the more intense and irrational the reaction appears, the more likely there is an earlier emotional or traumatic memory that has been activated. The memory may be from early childhood, from parental misattunement, abuse, or neglect. On the other hand, the memory may stem from a prior wound in the couple's relationship itself (Johnson et al. 2001) or from wounds from other relationships or life experiences. Even as the therapist may be befuddled by the power of the reaction, so may the other partner, who might be thinking, "I just forgot to tell her I'd be a half hour late coming home. What's the big deal?" The big deal is that 10 years ago he had an affair; or that 20 years ago her father had a sudden heart attack and died. Or, a client may not recall having been sexually abused repeatedly as a child, yet panics when approached for sex today by the spouse. The power of these emotional memories, and the hold they can have on us, is often perplexing and upsetting to all involved.

These emotional memories tend to be processed and "remembered" in the amygdala, a part of the limbic (emotional) brain that we share with other mammals. In evolutionary terms, the amygdala functions to protect our survival; it is one of the brain areas that mediate the fight-or-flight response. The amygdala scans the environment for danger; its quick work is done without consulting the higher brain processes of the prefrontal cortex. The amygdala can identify a snake in the woods and prompt us to run before we even know that we are seeing a snake (or what passes for a snake but is really a shadow or a stick). This survival function is obviously crucial in the woods, in a dark alley, or any unsafe circumstance. However, our amygdala doesn't know that now we are in a mature love relationship and our lives are not necessarily at stake when we get hurt. When the amygdala gets a whiff of threat, it sends our bodies into high gear before we have a moment to collect ourselves. This is the neurobiological underpinning of the escalation in the couple therapist's office.

Our sense of threat in an intimate relationship is not always a distortion, however. There are certainly real dangers—of physical or emotional abuse, for example—

that must be addressed on their own terms. Even in these circumstances, in addition to maximizing safety, the therapist may need to help clients harness their "thinking brains" to evaluate, plan, and respond most successfully.

As humans, we are blessed not just with an amygdala, but also with more complex brain functions for processing our emotional lives. Among the gear with which we are outfitted is the prefrontal cortex (PFC), the seat of reasoning, reflection, and judgment. It is the PFC that we call upon as therapists—both our own and the partners' PFCs. When we ask couples to take a time out, breathe, meditate, reflect, or journal, we are calling on this part of the brain. The PFC—especially the orbitofrontal cortex—is wired to communicate with the amygdala and calm it down. For some clients, the PFC underfunctions due to a history of early abuse or neglect, which can actually damage brain circuits. Furthermore, even in a healthy brain, the links from amygdala up to PFC are stronger than from PFC to amygdala (LeDoux 1996). Thus we so often experience meltdowns, moments when our higher brains are not in control, and we are at the mercy of our emotional reactivity.

The PFC has been called the "high road" (LeDoux 1996; Siegel and Hartzell 2003) as it allows us to make thoughtful choices—and also because it is located higher in the brain and developed more recently in evolution. The "low road" is identified with limbic functioning, often the amygdala, and involves automatic appraisals, outside of awareness, that can lead to impulsive, reactive behavior (LeDoux 1996; Siegel and Hartzell 2003). The "low road" language sounds a bit disparaging of our emotional/limbic brain, which, in fact, is crucial for social processing, including such skills as nonconscious empathy (Damasio 1994; Gladwell 2005). What is most important for healthy functioning is integration, the ability to coordinate limbic system and PFC, left and right hemispheres, thought and feeling, mind and body (Siegel 2007).

The amygdala is "quick to learn and slow to forget" (Cozolino 2006, p. 318). It holds emotional memories, probably forever (LeDoux 1996). Therapy and healing, then, do not entail erasing painful memories in the amygdala. Rather, what is involved is strengthening the PFC and its connections to the amygdala, so we can learn to self-soothe and self-regulate even in moments of stress, when the amygdala is activated.

For many clients, both self-attunement—reading their own emotions—and self-soothing are impossible tasks. They may have never learned to read emotions, their own or others', and due to misattuned, abusive, or overindulgent early family experiences, may not know how to self-regulate or calm themselves when upset. Instead, such clients often look to their partners to calm them down, to understand, hold, and love them, even when they are most difficult and attacking. Clients tend to be hurt when their partners disappoint in this job description. Teaching such clients how to self-regulate is empowering for the individual and vital for the couple's well-being.

Using imagery can be a useful technique to help clients learn to calm down when agitated. Specifically, I ask clients to image their amygdala getting worked up, and their PFC coming in like a good parent to empathically contain and soothe the amygdala. This process is similar to Schwartz's (1995) Internal Family Systems (IFS) approach, in which the therapist promotes a dialogue within the client between Self and parts. If clients have a hard time enlisting their loving Self/PFC to soothe themselves, yet are relatively empathic with their own (actual) child, I ask them to imagine calming their upset inner child as if it were their own child. Clients appreciate this work, as it empowers them to access a more compassionate state within themselves. As with IFS parts work, clients come to see that they are not one with their dysfunction, that when a part of their brain is stirred up, another, soothing part can be called upon. Like externalization (White and Epston 1990), this process helps free clients from a sense of shame, promotes curiosity, and allows for a new story of the self to emerge.

Another imagery technique I have developed is "the fence exercise" (Fishbane 2005). For example, in the course of couple therapy, it emerges that Maria loses herself and becomes agitated when her husband or mother becomes anxious or sad. Maria tries to make them feel better; when she fails, she gets angry at them. Maria's boundaries are highly porous in both relationships. I ask Maria to imagine that her mother is her neighbor, with a fence between their yards. The fence is not a brick barricade; like most fences, it is in part symbolic. While one can see over it, it demarcates a boundary between the two yards. I suggest that if the neighbor gardens in a way that Maria feels is problematic—putting sun-loving flowers in the shade, for instance—Maria may or may not choose to offer advice to the neighbor. But if the neighbor ignores the advice, Maria can still enjoy her own garden; her summer doesn't have to be ruined because of her neighbor's horticultural mistakes. If, of course, the neighbor plants poison ivy that will creep into Maria's yard, Maria needs to protect herself. Clients find this exercise helpful. Maria reports to me, "I put my mother on her side of the fence this week"; Maria was able to let her mother be without losing her own footing. As she developed greater differentiation (Bowen 1978) and self-regulation, Maria became less angry and more compassionate toward her mother and husband, and she was able to stay calm in the face of their turbulence. The fence exercise facilitates healthy boundaries and from that place clients can afford to be more generous and curious in their intimate relationships.

Research has shown that imagining doing an activity can activate the same neural circuits as actually doing the activity (Doidge 2007). I would hypothesize that both the imagined PFC/amygdala dialogue and the fence exercise activate brain circuits of reflection and thoughtfulness that allow the client to take a step back from automatic reactivity, and that through these and other practices, synaptic connections between PFC and amygdala are indeed being strengthened. If this is the case, then conjuring the image of brain circuitry can help create and strengthen that very circuitry. In any case, it certainly helps clients make more thoughtful choices and feel less victimized in their intimate relationships.

This internal imagery work facilitates self-empathy, which includes being able to read one's own emotions. In the neuroscience literature, emotions are considered nonconscious and embodied; we "read" our own body's signals, and then give words to the experience. "Feelings" result from this conscious labeling of our body experience (LeDoux 1996). Many of the body cues come from our gut. The vagus nerve carries information from the gut to the brain, giving literal punch to the expression "gut feeling." Clients who have not learned to label their own emotions are handicapped in their relational lives. This is especially the case for men who have been socialized away from awareness of emotion and for members of both genders who were not raised with attunement. These clients may have sudden upsurges of rage without knowing why. In such cases I help clients tune into the prodromal body cues before the anger and learn to give words to these subtler emotions. Siegel (2007) suggests that mindfulness meditation facilitates "intrapersonal attunement," which he posits may utilize the same "resonance circuitry" in the brain as interpersonal attunement. Research shows the beneficial effect meditation can have, facilitating positive and resilient mood states (Davidson 2004; Siegel 2007).

In addition to self-empathy, we help couples in therapy develop greater empathy for each other. The neuroscience literature has much to say about this interpersonal resonance. The human brain is wired to attune to others, to read social cues, facial expressions, and the intentions of our fellow humans. These capacities are considered part of our evolutionary survival mechanism; they utilize the social circuits of the emotional brain. Among the more fascinating discoveries in recent years are "mirror neurons," which activate a resonance in our brain when we see someone else do or feel something. Through this process we can feel what another feels "from the inside out" (Siegel and Hartzell 2003).

One of the most delightful aspects of falling in love is looking in our lover's eyes and "feeling felt" (Siegel and Hartzell 2003), understood, and cherished. Unfortunately, couples seeking therapy have often lost that magic mirroring; looking into each other's eyes, they see instead disconfirmation and rejection. Part of our work is to help the partners see each other with more generous eyes. Facilitating empathy and helping clients calm their amygdala go hand in hand in therapy. Just a look from one's partner can set off alarm bells that lead to the low road and that block empathy entirely. I find that interventions like the Speaker/Listener technique facilitate both calm and empathy as partners learn to listen to each other in dialogue rather than prepare their rebuttal in debate. The shift in the room is palpable as each partner moves from self-protective modes of discourse to openness to the other. Eye contact in this exercise is key; hopefully partners are conveying in their eyes a desire to understand—a remnant of their initial, loving mirroring—rather than the piercing glance of enmity with which they may have come to the session.

Some clients find empathy a foreign language. The person learning empathy may work his or her way through the left brain to try to understand the other. For example, a husband, struggling to understand his wife's experience, might learn to say to himself, "If I were my wife right now, with all I know about her, how might I be feeling?" This process may frustrate the partner, to whom this seems artificial, wooden, and painfully slow. Using a "neuroeducational" approach, I normalize the awkwardness and slow pace of the learner, as well as the frustration of the partner, thus validating the experience of both. Framing empathy as a skill that can be learned is reassuring to both partners. Atkinson (2005) refers to therapists as coaches, teachers of "emotional literacy." I find that eventually clients get the hang of empathy more naturally as their brains rewire for more efficient, less effortful attunement.

Looking into our partner's eyes and feeling what they feel is not always salutary. What we find there may send us into reactive orbit. Neuroscience has shown that our ability to resonate with others, to feel what they feel, is a mixed blessing. Due to "emotional contagion" (Goleman 2006), we can be driven into reactivity by others. Perhaps mirror neurons are implicated in this as well. Witnessing our partner become angry, defensive, or accusatory may activate similar circuits in our own brains, leading to escalations such as our struggling couple in the opening of this essay. Partners set each other off as they escalate into a "dance of parts" (Fishbane and Leasing 2000).

There are serious health implications of our ability to drive each other into agitated states. Gottman's "limbic tango" (Goleman 1995, p. 141) describes the dance of a wife raising conflictual issues, leading to escalation of the husband's heart rate and physiological flooding, leading to his shutdown or stonewalling, leading to her distressed heart rate. This all happens in an instant, and can result in long-term emotional and physical distress for one or both. Research identifies that nurturing relationships promote physical and mental health, while "toxic relationships are as major a risk factor for disease and death as are smoking, high blood pressure, or cholesterol, obesity, and physical inactivity" (Goleman 2006, p. 224). Clearly, the stakes in relationships are very high.

The skills of empathy and self-empathy are components of relationship empowerment, which includes Goleman's notions of emotional and social intelligence (1995, 2006). In facilitating relational empowerment, I offer clients "tools for your toolbox" (Fishbane 2007), specific social/emotional skills that engage the other in a mutually respectful manner. Men are particularly appreciative of the "tools" and empowerment language, as many males are suspicious of therapy as a "soft," female endeavor, for the weak and vulnerable. Men are often at a disadvantage in relationships, not having learned to read others' or their own emotions. Framing these tools as skills to be mastered makes the project manageable as we operationalize specific abilities that increase the client's relational competence. I find that when clients feel relationally empowered, they are less likely to resort to "power over" tactics with their partner.

As one of these relational tools, I encourage partners to learn how to "make a relational claim" (Fishbane 2001) with each other. This entails speaking one's needs, while holding the needs of the other and of the relationship at the same time. It means having a voice without obliterating the other. Given that our culture encourages debate rather than dialogue, it is not surprising that so many couples don't know how to do this. In teaching skills of dialogue, we are challenging the "power over" assumptions many couples hold in their relationships, in which win/lose negotiations dominate. While recognizing power differences—based in financial, physical power, or other differentials—I also introduce the idea of "power to" (Goodrich 1991) and "power with" (Jordan et al. 1991). "Power to" includes self-mastery, the ability to be thoughtful in one's relational life. It is epitomized by the Roman stoic philosopher Seneca's statement, "He is most powerful who has power over himself" (Seneca n.d.). "Power to" requires integration of higher and lower brain regions, bringing thoughtfulness and emotion together. It bears much in common with differentiation of self. "Power with" reflects a mutuality of concern, and the nonzero sum game that is crucial to a successful intimate relationship.

When partners do get reactive or defensive with each other, I use "news from neuroscience" to normalize this reaction as part of our evolutionary brain heritage when we feel attacked. At the same time, I challenge clients to call upon their higher brain functions so they are not at the mercy of their own instinctual reactions. This combination of normalizing and challenging is crucial in my work with couples. For example, in exploring a couple's vulnerability cycle (Scheinkman and Fishbane 2004), I identify their mutually recursive vulnerabilities and survival strategies. While normalizing self-protective mechanisms such as criticism and withdrawal when a partner feels vulnerable, I also point out the self-defeating nature of these mechanisms. Externalizing the couple's dance and each partner's survival strategies allows for greater empathy, thoughtfulness, and choice.

Along with "neuroeducation," I explore with couples the natural life cycle of relationships and their shifting neurobiological characteristics. According to Fisher (2004), there are three distinct phases in love relationships, each with its own brain circuitry and hormones, and each with its own evolutionary purpose. She denotes these as Lust, fired mostly by testosterone, whose purpose is to get people interested in mating in general; Romantic Love, powered by dopamine and norepinephrine, whose purpose is to settle on a particular mate; and Attachment, fueled by oxytocin and vasopressin, whose purpose is to keep the parents together long enough to rear their young beyond infancy. (Fisher doesn't address how this evolutionary paradigm would apply to childless couples.)

In addition to helping couples understand the normal processes of the life cycle of love, I reframe disconnection as a normative relationship process. Connection and disconnection, rupture and repair, are part of the natural ebb and flow in any intimate relationship. Gottman's (1999) research, for example, shows that both happy and unhappy couples experience conflict and it is how the happy couples repair their conflicts that distinguish them from unhappy couples. Framing repair and apology as part of relational intelligence and relational power rather than as indices of "losing" a fight is crucial for couples. Apology is a major tool in the relational toolbox. Gottman's 20-minute rule—that couples should take a break when in an angry escalation and reunite after they have calmed down—makes neurobiological sense. The couple return to each other without their inflamed amygdalas running the show.

Couple therapists deal with the tension between change and no-change with our clients. Our field has produced tomes on the topic of "resistance." Neuroscience sheds light on this dynamic so central to our work. On the one hand, habits and personality characteristics are formed early in life, and are reflected in brain wiring. Hebb's Law, "neurons that fire together wire together" (Siegel 1999, p. 26), captures the neuronal basis for the tenacity of our habits. The more we do, think, or feel something, the more likely we are to do so in the future. We literally become stuck in our own neuronal ruts. While this is adaptive much of the time, in that so much of our functioning is automatic and smooth, it is also the basis for the difficulty in overcoming unproductive habits and behaviors.

On the other hand, we are not doomed perennially to repeat the past. In the last decade, it has become clear that the adult brain can and does change. Neuroplasticity (the creation of new neuronal connections) and neurogenesis (the growth of new neurons) allow us to change throughout the life cycle (Begley 2007; Doidge 2007). This is the neural basis for our business, the process of change in therapy. I find it helpful to share the news both of Hebb's Law and of neuroplasticity with clients who are struggling with change. When a client asks, "Can an old dog learn new tricks? Can I change?", I have an intelligent answer based in neuroscience. The answer is yes, but it requires a lot of effort and repetition of new habits; "massed practice" is a vital condition of rewiring in the human brain (Doidge 2007). For new neuronal connections to take hold via Hebb's Law, the new behaviors need to be practiced over and over again until they become automatic. In times of stress, fatigue, or illness, the old patterns may re-emerge. Anticipating this helps clients not become discouraged with their own backsliding. Our role as therapists includes lending hope to clients. The hope we offer about change is tempered with a reliance on practice and overlearning of new habits so they can become natural.

Some clients are suspicious of behaviors, thoughts, or feelings that seem artificial, not natural, or "from the heart." I explain that new behaviors, which both create and are maintained by new neuronal connections, will feel awkward at first, until they are overlearned. Eventually, they will feel natural as they become automatic. This "love (or change) takes work" philosophy comes as a surprise to some clients, who subscribe to a "love should just flow" or "love means never having to say you're sorry" philosophy.

When changes do take hold, the new behaviors and skills are reflected in changes in the brain. Neuroscientists note that learning—including the learning at the heart of psychotherapy—involves new neuronal connections (Doidge 2007; Kandel 1998). This helps explain the phenomenon I often experience with clients, that changes they are working on in one relationship—say, with a spouse—carry over into other relationships—for example, with parents, child, or boss. The changes of self in relationship become synergistic, as the client builds on new capacities in different contexts.

Couple therapy that utilizes interpersonal neurobiology facilitates "limbic revision" (Lewis et al. 2000), a rewiring of the emotional brain. This is not about simple behavior change, nor is it achieved through strategic manipulation. It is deep, collaborative work, based on safety and respect. Clients feel they can risk limbic change when they feel accepted and respected rather than shamed or blamed by the therapist. Partners are encouraged to develop a new, more generous stance with each other as well.

The approach to couple therapy described here is based on a collaborative relationship between therapist and clients. Neuroeducation facilitates a transparency in the work, in which therapist and couple work as partners for change. Teaching clients about their own brain functioning is empowering. The constantly evolving field of interpersonal neurobiology can enhance our work as couple therapists, deepening our understanding of the profoundly social nature of the human being, and pointing to clinical interventions that help both couple and therapist make informed choices.

This work helps clients and therapists feel less overwhelmed by the reactivity in the room, and more capable of facilitating and maintaining change.

References

Atkinson, B. (2005). *Emotional intelligence in couples therapy: Advances from neurobiology and the science of intimate relationships*. New York, NY: W.W. Norton.

Begley, S. (2007). *Train your mind, change your brain*. New York, NY: Ballantine.

Bowen, M. (1978). *Family therapy in clinical practice*. New York, NY: Jason Aronson.

Cozolino, L. J. (2006). *The neuroscience of relationships: Attachment and the developing social brain*. New York, NY: W.W. Norton.

Damasio, A. (1994). *Descartes' error: Emotion, reason, and the human brain*. New York, NY: Penguin.

Davidson, R. J. (2004). Well-being and affective style: Neural substrates and biobehavioral correlates. *Philosophical Transactions Royal Society of London, 359*, 1395–1411.

Doidge, N. (2007). *The brain that changes itself*. New York, NY: Viking.

Fishbane, M. D. (2001). Relational narratives of the self. *Family Process, 40*, 273–291.

Fishbane, M. D. (2005). Differentiation and dialogue in intergenerational relationships. In J. Lebow (Ed.), *Handbook of clinical family therapy* (pp. 543–568). Hoboken, NJ: John Wiley & Sons.

Fishbane, M. D. (2007). Wired to connect: Neuroscience, relationships, and therapy. *Family Process, 46,* 395–412.

Fishbane, M. D., & Leasing, B. (2000). The "dance of parts": Integrating IFS with psychodynamic, systemic, and relational approaches to couples therapy. Presentation at the Annual Internal Family Systems Conference, Evanston, IL.

Fisher, H. (2004). *Why we love: The nature & chemistry of romantic love*. New York, NY: Henry Holt.

Gladwell, M. (2005). *Blink: The power of thinking without thinking*. New York, NY: Little, Brown.

Goleman, D. (1995). *Emotional intelligence*. New York, NY: Bantam.

Goleman, D. (2006). *Social intelligence: The new science of human relationships*. New York, NY: Bantam.

Goodrich, T. J. (1991). Women, power and family therapy: What's wrong with this picture? In T. J. Goodrich (Ed.), *Women and power: perspectives for family therapy* (pp. 3–35). New York, NY: W. W. Norton.

Gottman, J. (1999). *The seven principles for making marriage work*. New York, NY: Crown.

Johnson, S. M., Makinen, J. A., & Millikin, J. W. (2001). Attachment injuries in couple relationships: A new perspective on impasses in couples therapy. *Journal of Marital & Family Therapy, 27,* 145–155.

Jordan, J. V., Kaplan, A. G., Miller, J. B., Stiver, I. P., & Surrey, J. L. (Eds.) (1991). *Women's growth in connection: Writings from the Stone Center* (pp. 51–66). New York: Guilford.

Kandel, E. R. (1998). A new intellectual framework for psychiatry. *American Journal of Psychiatry, 155,* 457–469.

LeDoux, J. (1996). *The emotional brain: The mysterious underpinnings of emotional life*. New York, NY: Simon & Schuster.

Lewis, T., Amini, F., & Lannon, R. (2000). *A general theory of love*. New York, NY: Vintage/Random House.

Scheinkman, M., & Fishbane, M. D. (2004). The vulnerability cycle: Working with impasses in couple therapy. *Family Process, 43,* 279–299.

Schore, A. (2003). *Affect regulation and the repair of the Self*. New York, NY: W. W. Norton.

Schwartz, R. C. (1995). *Internal family systems*. New York, NY: Guilford.

Seneca (n.d.). Letters to Lucilius, 90.34, Loeb Classical Library.

Siegel, D. (1999). *The developing mind: How relationships and the brain interact to shape who we are*. New York, NY: Guilford.
Siegel, D. J. (2007). *The mindful brain: Reflection and attunement in the cultivation of well-being*. New York, NY: W. W. Norton.
Siegel, D. J., & Hartzell, M. (2003). *Parenting from the inside out*. New York, NY: Penguin.
White, M., & Epston, D. (1990). *Narrative means to therapeutic ends*. New York, NY: Norton.

Neurobiology and Addiction: Assisting the Family and Support System to Get Resistant Loved Ones into Treatment

Judith Landau and James Garrett

> *"I drove through the neighborhood and I walked those mean streetsI begged those using buddies for the secrets they keepAnd I raged out at their silence and I almost lost controlNow I question my own sanity as I search deep within my soul.Where are our children tonight?"* From song: *Where Is My Child Tonight* by Steve Dan Mills, 2004

Living With a Stranger

Counselor:	Hello, may I help you?
Family Member:	Yes. I got your name from a friend who said you helped her family get their daughter into treatment. Do you do that type of work?
Counselor:	Yes, we work with families and others who care about the person with a problem to form a team designed to help get an individual with an addiction problem started in treatment.
Family Member:	Thank you. I have been calling everywhere and you are the first person who will actually talk with me about this. The other places only told me that they couldn't help until the person called in requesting help or they just wanted to refer me to Al-Anon.
Counselor:	Please tell me about the person you are concerned about.
Family Member:	I am calling about my 18-year-old son. He got arrested over the weekend for an open beer container in the car and possession of pot. This happened a week after he got suspended from school for leaving after his 1st period class with some of his loser friends.

Editors' note: First published in 2008, American Family Therapy Academy Monograph Series.

J. Landau (✉)
Linking Human Systems, LLC, Boulder, CO, USA
e-mail: jlandau@arise-network.com

LINC Foundation, Inc., Boulder, CO, USA

J. Garrett
Recovery Resource Center, Albany, NY, USA

T. Nelson, H. Winawer (eds.), *Critical Topics in Family Therapy*,
AFTA SpringerBriefs in Family Therapy, DOI 10.1007/978-3-319-03248-1_11,

Counselor: Have you seen any major changes in your son's behavior, attitude, school performance, and/or respect for you as parents, or other changes in his relationships?

Family Member: Major changes—that's an understatement! Our son was an honor roll student in 9th grade. He played two sports and was in the school play as a freshman. He was a delight to be around. Then, in his sophomore year, he began to drink on weekends. That next summer he began to smoke pot and last year turned out to be a disaster. He totally changed. He flunked three courses, quit sports, and became an angry, belligerent kid. We don't know him anymore!

Counselor: It sounds like this is not the son you raised and once knew.

Family Member: You are right. He has turned into a complete stranger. We have lost our son and we want to get him back. We're really scared about what's happening to him. We don't know him anymore.

Counselor: I understand. Your story is really typical of parents who say they are now living with a stranger. We can help you get your son back as you begin to understand what the addiction is doing to his brain and how the love and support of the family plays a most important role in getting him into treatment and supporting his recovery.

As the words in the song quoted above and the telephone dialogue of the parent talking about the stranger now living with the family so painfully describe: substance abuse and addiction hijack brain and the subsequent damage leads to increasingly intolerable circumstances. The inevitable progression of untreated addiction results in individuals becoming irrational, defiant, unpredictable, self-centered, and irresponsible. The people closest to them suffer the most hurt. These family members and concerned others are also the ones who most frequently call a treatment agency or therapist asking for assistance in getting their loved ones into treatment.

This paper explores the impact of active addiction on one area of the brain, the prefrontal cortex, as an illustration of the neurobiological effect of addiction. It describes how changes in identity of the active addict impact family and other significant relationships, leading to a perception of boundary ambiguity resulting from a situation of ambiguous loss very similar to that experienced by families dealing with Alzheimer's disease or Mild Traumatic Brain Injury (MTBI). The paper concludes with a description of an evidence-based best practice method designed to work with family members and concerned others to help get an addicted loved one (or other person not taking adequate measures to protect his or own physical or mental health) started in treatment.

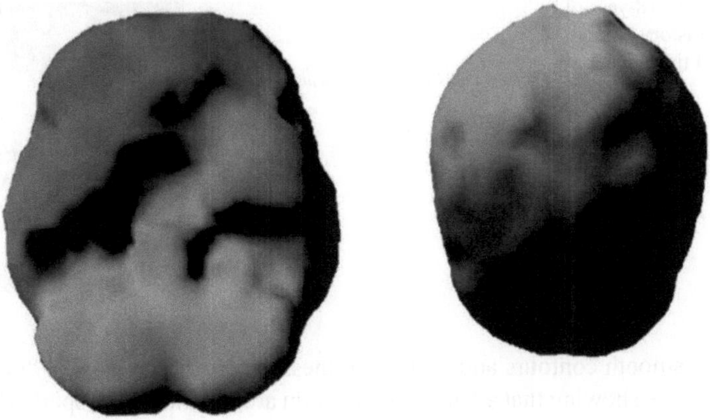

Normal, Healthy Brain—Top View

Normal, Healthy Brain—Bottom View

Fig. 1 SPECT Images of Normal, Healthy Brain

The Neurobiology of Addiction

The process of change and sense of loss experienced by the parent in the above phone call is typical after the onset of addiction (Landau and Garrett, in press, 2008). The experience is real and not imagined or an over-reaction. The vast majority of parents and spouses who call to get an addicted loved one into treatment report terrifying changes in personality, attitude, and behavior. The callers feel that they no longer know their loved ones and these changes are the most significant motivating factors behind reaching out for help. If the treating therapist understands the neurobiology of addiction and how addiction changes the brain and its function, the concern and loss that family members experience is validated, allowing them to develop strategies for dealing with the impact of the disease (Erikson and Wilcox 2001). Five sections of the brain are impacted by addiction: prefrontal cortex, limbic system, temporal lobes, anterior cingulate, and basal ganglia (Amen 1994). In this brief paper, we will describe the impact on only the prefrontal cortex to illustrate the disastrous effect of addiction on brain function.

Single Photon Emission Computerized Tomography (SPECT) provides a technology for studying brain function. SPECT imaging was developed in the late 1970s. It uses nuclear technology to study cerebral blood flow, an indicator of brain activity. SPECT images or brain maps are 3-D constructions by supercomputers that identify certain brain activity, often deep in the brain, that correspond to cognitive, behavioral, and emotional functioning. SPECT images document that addiction is not a problem of brain *structure*, but rather a problem of brain *function* or *lack of function* (Fig. 1).

Figure 1 images show a healthy, normal brain from both the top and bottom

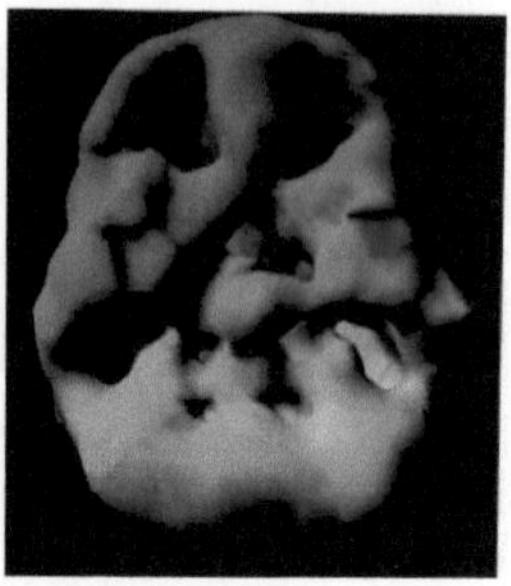

Fig. 2 Image of 18-year-old with 3-year history of marijuana use—4 times/week

Note the smooth contours and surface fullness. There are no gaps or "holes" in the brain image, showing that all areas of the brain are functioning properly (Fig. 2).

Figure 2 image shows the functional "holes" in the pre-frontal cortex of an 18-year-old who has been using cannabis four times a week since age 15. The First Call described above was from a parent about his 18-year-old son. This image shows how his son's brain is not functioning in a healthy way and has left the father "living with a stranger"

The prefrontal cortex is the first part of the brain affected by alcohol and other drugs. This is where the executive functions of judgment, impulse control (inhibitions), and self-monitoring are located, so it is not surprising that excessive use of alcohol and other drugs first impact judgment, inhibition, and rational thinking. It also augments the memory function of the temporal lobes, playing a major role in how memory is utilized as a learning tool that then appropriately guides and governs behavior (Nestler 2001).

The prefrontal cortex is also involved in a number of coping functions: attention span, organization, learning from experience, empathy, and problem solving. Malfunction of the prefrontal cortex due to addiction results in irrational thinking, inability objectively to assess oneself, self-centeredness, poor judgment, inability to learn from experience, disorganization, decreased attention span, becoming easily bored, short temper and argumentativeness, and becoming thin skinned (Hyman 1994).

The effects of alcohol/drugs on the brain can vary depending on the age of the person and the type of drug used. For instance, in the case example with the telephone dialogue at the start of the paper, the parent was calling in about her 18-year-old son. We know that the prefrontal cortex normally continues to develop through the teen years and into the early twenties. The immature and/or problematic behavior patterns typically associated with adolescence are directly related to prefrontal cortex maturation and function. When an underdeveloped prefrontal cortex is impacted by drugs and/or alcohol, the neurobiological effects are more quickly noticed. The longer the individual continues to abuse alcohol/drugs, the more developmental catching up that individual will have in later life. These are the adults who are described as perennial adolescents with poor impulse control and judgment, immature handling of situations and relationships, difficulty with authority figures, irresponsibility, and irrational decision making. The old recovery adage that states, "A person stops growing emotionally at the point where the addiction began" is validated by the newest SPECT images (NIH 2006).

The best prevention technique a parent can use to reduce the likelihood of addiction is to postpone their son or daughter's age of starting to use alcohol/drugs as long as possible—certainly until the age of 20. The older an individual is when she or he starts to abuse alcohol or drugs, the less likely this individual will ever experience an addiction problem, regardless of genetic predisposition. "People who reported starting to drink before the age of 15 were four times more likely to also report meeting the criteria for alcohol dependence at some point in their lives" (DeWit et al. 2000, pp. 745–750). These youngsters displayed problem-drinking patterns, using alcohol to "get high" rather than participating in what might be called culturally sanctioned social drinking with their parents (Grant and Dawson 1997).

The research shows that all psychoactive drugs impact the prefrontal cortex. Some drugs impact more quickly than others. For instance, cocaine has a much quicker and stronger impact on the prefrontal cortex than alcohol. It should also be noted that long-term neurobiological damage also differs by type of drug (Erikson 2007). For instance, methamphetamine, cocaine, and ecstasy have all been shown to have long-term (over 2 years) impact on the neural pathways of the brain, suggesting it would be more difficult successfully to treat addiction to these particular substances (NIDA Notes 2000). The rate of healing for the prefrontal cortex is dependent on such factors as the drug(s) of choice, the amount, and frequency of use, the length of use, and the age of the individual. Recent research indicates that it is necessary to have a minimum of 90 days of abstinence to show sufficient healing of the prefrontal cortex to return cognition, attitude, and self-assessment to a rational level of functioning (Lemonick 2007).

When family members understand that the effect of addiction on the brain provides a rationale for their experience, their concerns and sense of living with a stranger are validated. They are then able to mobilize their energies and increase their commitment to focus on the problems and take action. The family is motivated to start the process of motivating their addicted individual to enter treatment. A profound change has occurred and the family dares to hope that they can get their loved one back, rather than being overwhelmed by despair.

Identity and Ambiguous Loss in the Family

The injury to the brain from addiction is, in many ways, similar to other types of brain injuries that have a profound impact on family relationships. Extensive research on the relational impact of Alzheimer's disease has been documented (Boss 1999, 2006). Landau and Hissett (2008) describe the recent exploration of a similar process in the case of MTBI. Unless this process is recognized and dealt with in the relational setting, relational breakdown including problems with children and adolescents, marital problems, and divorce are likely to result.

In a very similar way, the loss of a loved one to the addictive process causes serious confusion because the person is still physically present, but is behaving very differently from the person the family knew and loved. The loved one's physical and emotional deficits profoundly alter their interactions with family and others. This change in identity of the addicted individual (with or without his or her awareness) creates a sense of boundary ambiguity in couples and families. This may manifest as loss of the addicted person as the family knew her or him, as well as loss of the family system as it once was. All the rules have suddenly changed and family members struggle to develop new boundaries and maintain effective communication. With such ambiguous loss, the boundary ambiguity is left unresolved. Since the addicted person is still present, family members do not recognize or grieve the loss of the loved one, and are often unable to heal and move on. Similarly to Seaburn's (1990) description of cancer as the unwelcome guest and Landau and Hissett's (2008) description of MTBI's becoming the dominant topic in a family where a member has suffered a head injury, families dealing with addiction frequently struggle with the realization that the disease "has left a stranger in their midst who has become the predominant presence in every conversation and major decision" (Landau and Garrett, in press, 2008).

Families dealing with addiction refrain from discussing their experiences to avoid alienation, blame, guilt, and shame. They "walk on egg shells," terrified of losing the addicted individual by dealing openly with the problem. This combination of ambiguity and secrecy compounds the problem. Clinically, these effects appear to be associated with considerable stress, and may correlate with the breakdown of couple, parent, and family relationships (Landau and Hissett, 2008). The person (usually the spouse or parent) living with an addicted person is likely to make frequent visits to the primary care provider's office with minor ailments, or to consult a therapist about depression and anxiety. Unless specifically asked about addiction in the family, the cause of the distress might never come to light as in the situation of Mrs. M. described below (Landau and Garrett, in press, 2008).

A 43-year-woman, Mrs. M., who had reluctantly requested therapy for depression and headaches, brought her 18-year-old daughter, Mary, and 15-year-old son, Jerry, to the first session with her. Mrs. M. explained that her husband was too busy at work to take the time to accompany them. While she described a happy, successful family, the teenagers pulled faces and at times smirked behind her back. Finally, as she described her husband in glowing terms, Jerry burst out, "If you're so happy, why are you always in bed with a migraine?" At this point, Mary said, "If you're not going to tell the story, I will." In total surprise, her mother asked, "What story?" "You have a headache every weekend when Dad comes home. The only time you do things with us, like going to movies or the pool, are the weekends he's away on business."

Mrs. M. looked stunned and explained that the changes in her husband's behavior were related to his overload in the office and his extensive travel as a result of promotion at work. She described how he frequently seemed to be distracted and that his concentration was not what it used to be. Jerry complained that he could no longer ask his father a simple question "without getting my head bitten off." Mrs. M. also said that he'd become somewhat moody and had been involved in a recent accident. Mother had not noticed any relationship between her migraines and her husband's behavior and felt that her depression was just a result of her age and hormonal situation.

On careful questioning about the gradual changes in Mr. M's behavior and habits, the family started to realize that he had begun to drink most Friday nights when he was home. In fact, sometimes, he even smelled of drink when he arrived. They had not associated this fact with any of the recent changes in him or in their family relationships. On further exploration, while Mrs. M. still rationalized his behavior in terms of his work situation, her daughter Mary sighed and said, "Gosh Mom, I hadn't realized until we put it together now how much he's been drinking. How could you not have noticed? He's not the dad I grew up with and he's not there for any of us anymore. He hasn't seen a single one of Jerry's football matches this year and he pushed him to play in the first place."

While the children had been disturbed by the changes in their father, mother had attributed all of them to his work situation. On careful assessment, it became apparent that father had been drinking increasingly heavily over the past year and was showing distinct signs of neurobiological damage. The family made a commitment to work with the therapist to motivate dad to accompany them to the next meeting and felt confident that he would do so in order to help his wife get better.

Addicted relationships are always fraught with guilt, shame, and blame, reinforced by a lack of societal understanding about the impact of addiction on the functioning of the family. Unspoken anger and helplessness of family members and concerned others increases as the addictive process causes deterioration of the brain, resulting in cognitive deficit, reduction in rational thought, decreased responsibility, and increased impetuousness. These factors further reduce the addicted individual's insight and motivation to stop using. Denial prevails.

Fewer than 10 % of individuals addicted to substances ever get into treatment. The family is a neglected but critical source of motivation for treatment entry and maintaining the individual in treatment. In fact, the only path to long-term recovery is through family recovery, not just individual recovery. Alcoholism affects the family and the family can positively affect recovery from alcoholism. Helping members of the family and extended support system to understand the role of neurobiology in addiction reduces their ambivalence about the changes in their loved ones and allows them to focus on this disease with knowledge and hope.

Practical Implications for Clinicians Answering a Family Member's Request to Help a Resistant Loved One Getting Into Treatment

Overview of Invitational Intervention: The ARISE Model

Addiction kidnaps not only the addicted individual but holds the family for ransom with its overwhelming power. The ARISE Model (A Relational Intervention

Sequence for Engagement) mobilizes family and concerned others to motivate the addicted individual into treatment while moving the family as a whole into recovery. ARISE is a three-level, pre-treatment, engagement process based on openness and a commitment to honor and maintain the investment and connectedness of families. The ARISE model has no surprises or secrets. The ARISE Interventionist is present (either in person or on the telephone) for all meetings. The family and support system take a very active role in the intervention process. This minimizes the clinician's expenditure of time and cost and empowers the family, overcoming their blame, shame, and guilt. The Invitational Intervention method stops at the first level where the addicted individual enters treatment. The principle of ARISE is to stop at the first level that works, thereby minimizing the time and effort of the outside professional—the ARISE Interventionist—as well as drawing on the resilience of the family and giving them back the power that the addiction has usurped.

Level 1 uses motivational techniques designed specifically for telephone coaching, but can also be applied in face-to-face sessions. The ARISE interventionist helps the "First Caller" or "Concerned Other" establish a basis of hope, identify whom to invite to the initial intervention meeting, design a strategy to mobilize the support group, teach techniques to successfully invite the alcohol-dependent or addicted individual to the first meeting, suggest a recovery message (based on the intergenerational story of loss and on the neurobiological damage to the brain), and get a commitment from all invited individuals to attend the initial meeting regardless of whether or not the alcoholic attends. Level 1 comprises the First Call and The First Meeting. The ARISE Interventionist conducts both, while encouraging the First Caller and Intervention Network to take a central role in the decision-making and motivating the addicted individual to enter treatment.

In a recent study, over 55 % of the 110 substance abusers in the study sample entered treatment during Level 1 (Landau et al. 2004). Concerns about the loss of the loved one as the family once knew him or her always comes up during the First Call. The protocol includes questions about changes in cognition, responsibility, attitude, behavioral functioning, and relationships and builds on the interest of the First Caller in getting the loved one back (Landau and Garrett, in press, 2008). The ARISE Interventionist validates the changes described by the First Caller with solid scientific information relating the neurobiological process of addiction to the specific changes reported. The First Caller generally experiences a sense of immediate relief and begins to hope that recovery might be possible. Once this has occurred, the First Caller is in a far stronger position to mobilize the rest of the family and support network to motivate the addicted individual into treatment (Garrett et al. 1999).

Level 2 follows if treatment does not start during Level 1. Typically in Level 2, two to five face-to-face sessions are held, with or without the alcohol-dependent or addicted individual present, to mobilize the Intervention Network in developing motivational strategies to attain the goal of treatment engagement. Very few families (fewer than 2 %) need to proceed to level 3 (Landau et al. 2000).

In *Level 3*, family and friends set limits and consequences for the alcohol-dependent or addicted individual in a loving and supportive way. By the time the Intervention Network gets to this point, the alcohol-dependent or addicted individual has been given and has refused many opportunities to enter treatment. Because the alcohol-dependent or addicted individual has been invited to each of the Intervention Network meetings in Levels 1 and 2, this final limit-setting approach is a natural consequence and does not come as a surprise. The Intervention Network commits to supporting each other in the implementation of the agreed upon consequences (Garrett 1997).

Outcome data on ARISE (NIDA study DA09402) demonstrated that 83 % of addicted individuals entered treatment as the result of families' using the Invitational Intervention approach (Landau et al. 2004). There was no significant difference in severity of the addiction, drug of choice, or level of experience of the ARISE Interventionist. The average time taken per intervention was less than 90 min (average 88 min; median 75 min).

Summary

There is clear evidence that alcohol and drugs cause severe damage to the brain. The earlier the age of onset, the greater is the damage to the brain and the likelihood of the development of addiction. These neurobiological changes have a profound impact on the behavior and personality of the addicted individual to the extent that those closest to him or her feel that they are living with a stranger. Unless this process of deterioration is recognized and the resulting ambiguous loss is dealt with in the relational setting, relational breakdown is likely to result. Early recognition and treatment are essential for promoting brain recovery and for maintaining important relationships.

One of the most effective methods of ensuring that this occurs is to develop outreach programs offering the Invitational Intervention as a way of educating and mobilizing families and concerned others to motivate their addicted loved ones into treatment. *Invitational Intervention: The ARISE Model* is used in illustration of this process. ARISE works particularly well because it enables families to get a high percentage of their addicted individuals into treatment. It maintains positive connections with family and support systems well into the recovery period, focusing not only on individual recovery but also on family recovery (Fernandez et al. 2006).

The authors also encourage readers to utilize some of the following references for psychoeducational purposes when working with family members and/or addicted individuals:

- www.pubs.niaaa.nih.gov/publications/arh21–2/101.pdf
- www.nature.com/neuro/focus/addiction/index
- www.druginfo.nsw.gov.au/information_&_resources/addiction_and_neurobiology
- Addiction is a Brain Disease, and It Matters. www.drugabuse.gov/scienceofaddiction
- Levine, R. R., Walsh, C. A., and Schwartz, R. D. (1996). *Pharmacology: Drug actions and reactions.* New York, NY: Parthenon Publishing Group.

References

Amen, D. (1994). New directions in the theory, diagnosis, and treatment of mental disorders: The use of SPECT imaging in everyday clinical practice. In L. F. Koziol & C. E. Stout (Eds.) *the Neuropsychological of mental disorders* (pp. 286–311). Springfield, IL: Charles Thomas.

Boss, P. (1999). *Ambiguous loss: Learning to live with unresolved grief.* Cambridge, MA: Harvard University Press.

Boss, P. (2006). *Loss, trauma, and resilience: Therapeutic work with ambiguous loss.* New York: W. W. Norton.

DeWit, D., Adlaf, E., Offord, D., & Ogborne, A. (2000). Age at first alcohol use: A risk factor for the development of alcohol disorders. *American Journal of Psychiatry, 157,* 745–750.

Erikson, C. K. (2007). *The science of addiction.* New York, NY: W.W. Norton.

Erikson, C. K., & Wilcox, R. E. (2001). Neurobiological causes of addiction. *Journal of Social Work and Practice on Addictions, 1,* 7–22.

Fernandez, A. C., Begley, E. A., & Marlatt, G. A. (2006). Family and peer interventions for adults: Past approaches and future directions. *Psychology of Addictive Behaviors, 20,* 207–213.

Garrett, J., Landau, J., Stanton, M. D., Baciewicz, G., Shea, R., & Brinkman-Sull, D. (1999). The "concerned other" call: Using family links and networks to overcome resistance to addiction treatment. *Substance Use and Misuse, 34,* 363–382.

Grant, B. F., & Dawson, D. A. (1997). Age at onset of alcohol use and its association with DSM-IV alcohol abuse and dependence: Results from the national longitudinal alcohol epidemiologic survey. *Journal of Substance Abuse, 9,* 103–110.

Hyman, S. E. (1994). Why does the brain prefer opium to broccoli? *Harvard Review of Psychiatry, 2,* 43–63.

Landau, J., & Garrett, J. (in press, 2008). *Invitational intervention: A step-by-step guide for clinicians helping families engage resistant substance abusers in treatment.* Binghamton, NY: Haworth Press.

Landau, J., Garrett, J., Shear, R., Stanton, M. D., Brinkman-Sull, D., & Baciewicz, G. (2000). Strength in numbers: The ARISE method for mobilizing family and network to engage substance abusers in treatment. *American Journal of Drug and Alcohol Abuse, 26,* 379–398.

Landau, J., Stanton, M. D., Brinkman-Sull, D., Ikle, D., McCormick, D., Garrett, J., Baciewicz, G., Shea, R., & Wamboldt, F. (2004). Outcomes with the ARISE approach to engaging reluctant drug- and alcohol-dependent individuals in treatment. *American Journal of Drug and Alcohol Abuse, 30,* 711–748.

Landau, J., & Hissett, J. (2008). Mild traumatic brain injury: Impact on identity and ambiguous loss in the family. *Families Systems and Health, 26*(1), 69–85.

Lemonick, M. (2007, July 5). How we get addicted. *Time Magazine* [on-line]. http://www.time.com/time/magazine/article/0,9171,1640436,00.html?imw=Y. Accessed 10 Dec 2007.

Nestler, E. J. (2001). Total recall—the memory of addiction. *Science, 292,* 2266–2267.

Seaburn, D. B. (1990). *The unwelcome guest: Cancer joins children, parents, and grandparents. Plenary presented at Cancer: The family experience.* Cleveland, OH: University of Ireland Cancer Center.

Part V

Expanding Our social Justice Practices: Advances in Theory and Training, 2010 —Jane Ariel, Pilar Hernandez-Wolfe, and Sarah Stearns, Guest Editors

Doing Family: Decentering Heteronormativity in "Marriage" and "Family" Therapy

Jacqueline Hudak and Shawn V. Giammattei

Introduction

What would family therapy teaching and training look like if we were to deconstruct the core concept of family? In this essay, we begin that conversation by addressing the issue of heteronormativity and the profound impact it has upon the ways we think about and legitimize relationships.

The words, *marriage* and *family*, the nomenclature of our profession, are central to some of the most fiercely debated issues of our time. Despite the increased visibility of gay men and lesbian women, and the increasingly younger ages at which youth "come out" (Savin-Williams 2005; Tanner and Lyness 2003), there remains no definition of "family" in the public consciousness that refers to same-sex couples with children. In fact, in the not too distant past, the notions of lesbian mother, gay father or lesbian/gay family would have been nonexistent and the constitutive terms seen as mutually exclusive. We are further challenged to incorporate the discourses of a younger generation that refuses to define itself within the binary construction of sexual identity and chooses instead to live out narratives of queerness, heteroflexibility, ambisexuality (Morris 2006; Savin-Williams 2005). Current research (Diamond 2008a, b) compels us to incorporate the idea of sexual fluidity into our thinking about life trajectories.

In contrast to these cultural shifts, our field continues to engage in heteronormative discourses seen clearly, for example, by the frequency with which the language of "marriage," "couple," and "family" is used in theory, training, and conference plenaries without naming heterosexuality. As postmodern theorists have posited, attention must be given to the importance of cultural discourses and language as

Editors' note: First published in 2010, American Family Therapy Academy Monograph Series.

J. Hudak (✉)
University of Pennsylvania, Philadelphia, PA, USA
e-mail: jack4fta@comcast.net

S. V. Giammattei
San Francisco and Santa Rosa, CA, USA

T. Nelson, H. Winawer (eds.), *Critical Topics in Family Therapy*,
AFTA SpringerBriefs in Family Therapy, DOI 10.1007/978-3-319-03248-1_12,

they shape and impact the conception of both reality and legitimacy (Bruner 2002; Flax 1990; Harding 1990; Hare-Mustin 1994, 2004; Lather 1992). What is silenced or left unsaid is of tremendous consequence. As Hare-Mustin (1994) stated, "We do not only use language, it uses us. Language is recursive: it provides the categories in which we think" (p. 22).

This silence around heterosexuality maintains it as the default position, a position of dominance and superiority. For example, the descriptive terms, "couple" or "family" refer to heterosexual couples or heterosexual families. Couples and families who are "gay" or "lesbian" have to be named as such because otherwise they are invisible. Within these heteronormative discourses, heterosexuality and heterosexual forms of relating are considered the norm. This maintains the illusion that only LGBT individuals have a sexual orientation and that it is unnecessary to examine the development of heterosexuality.

As postmodern, feminist family therapists, we begin by situating ourselves in relation to this work. I (Jacqueline), one of the authors, am a second generation, European-American, middle-class woman who has practiced and taught family therapy since the early 1990s, always with a focus on issues of gender, power, diversity and social justice. I was in a heterosexual marriage for 13 years and am the mother of two children. In my mid-forties, I divorced and became partnered with a woman, necessitating that I "come out" to my children, family, and community.

I (Shawn), the other author, am a second generation Italian-American, upper middle-class married man who has practiced family therapy since 2000. I have been teaching family therapy and specifically about lesbian, gay, bisexual, and transgender issues in therapy since 2002. Similar to Jacqueline's, my work always has a focus on gender, power, diversity, community, and social justice. I have identified with the LGBT community since I was very young, but have spent many years trying to be "normal and straight" for my family. I have had long-term, significant relationships over the years with people of different genders.

If pushed to choose a category, each of us would identify as queer because that best represents the fluidity of our life trajectories and who we are today.

Heteronormativity

We contend that heteronormativity, defined as the dominant and pervasive belief that a viable family consists of a heterosexual mother and father raising heterosexual children together (Gamson 2000) is an organizing principle that shapes and constrains family therapy theory, practice, research, and training. Perlesz et al. (2006) make the following distinction between it and heterosexism: "We have defined heteronormativity as the uncritical adoption of heterosexuality as an established norm or standard. Heterosexism is the system by which heterosexuality is assumed to be the only acceptable and viable life option and hence to be superior, more natural and dominant" (p. 183). Aptly described by Oswald et al. (2005) as a "vast matrix of cultural beliefs, rules, rewards, privileges and sanctions" (p. 144), heteronormativity is buttressed by claims about what is considered "normal" and "healthy" for individuals, couples, and families.

Heteronormativity sustains the dominant norm of heterosexuality by rendering marginal any relational structure that falls outside of this "norm." Further, heteronormativity renders the diversity of human sexuality and identities invisible. This invisibility is marked by the fact that there is limited language to describe sexual minority experience and identities within dominant discourses. This creates a category of "other" in our culture, which is rendered invalid or pathological. What little language there is often creates false binary systems that are inaccurate representations of the actual lived experiences of many individuals. Given this lack of language, we often are left with the antiquated and imprecise categories of lesbian, gay, bisexual, and transgender (LGBT).

The heteronormative presumption, that everyone is heterosexual unless proven otherwise, is best expressed by the concept of "the closet," a metaphor for keeping one's sexual orientation and/or gender or sexual identity a secret. Sedgwick (1990) referred to "the closet" as "the defining structure for gay oppression in this century" (p. 71). Yoshino (2006) described it beautifully: "It was impossible to come out and be done with it, as each new person erected a new closet around me" (pp. 16–17).

Gender, Sexuality and Family

Intrinsic to heteronormative assumptions are ideas about "correct" or "normal" gender, sexuality, and family. Oswald and colleagues (2005) point out that it is the combination of these three structural components that constitute heteronormativity as a system of privilege. Oswald and colleagues stated, "Heteronormativity entails a convergence of at least three binary opposites: 'real' males and 'real' females versus gender 'deviants,' 'natural' sexuality versus 'unnatural' sexuality, and 'genuine' families versus 'pseudo families" (p. 144). The construction of binary opposites creates the illusion of an actual boundary between various genders and identities and privileges one side over the other. Gender, sexuality, and family are intrinsically linked, and as Oswald and colleagues stated, "Doing sexuality and doing family properly are inseparable from doing gender properly" (p. 144). All of the markers of adulthood—dating, marriage, and parenting—are traditionally tied to heterosexuality. Adult competencies associated with heterosexuality are distributed on the basis of gender (Spaulding 1999). Achieving mature adult status is most commonly measured by milestones that are linked to traditional heterosexual gender roles and behaviors.

The transformative use of gender as a verb is worth noting, as it was important in breaking down essentialist and binary assumptions about masculinity and femininity. Queer theorist Judith Butler (1990) introduced the notion of gender as an act or performance rather than a quality intrinsic to one's inherent nature. In this paradigm, gender is what you do at particular times rather than a universal of who you are. Historically it was believed that people were "inherently" male or female, gay or straight and each of these was dichotomously opposed to its counterpart (Fausto-Sterling 2000). This essentialist narrative of gender and sexuality continues to be a powerful and privileged narrative in our culture (Fausto-Sterling 2000; Laird 2003).

Sexual Minority Status

Dominant definitions of relationship and family have historically not included "sexual minorities." While gay men and lesbians are more visible in the family therapy literature, they still occupy the status of members in a minority group. Although it is not within the scope of this article to deal with all aspects of identity politics for LGBT families, certain facets of that politic are governed by heteronormative assumptions. The positioning of LGBT people as a minority group is one of the fixtures of heteronormative culture and thus merits further attention.

It is important to acknowledge the significant gains and scholarship in the field of marriage and family therapy regarding the inclusion of gay and lesbian couples and families in the literature. Since the publication of reviews that documented the omission of gay and lesbian issues in the marriage and family therapy field (Allen and Demo 1995; Clark and Serovich 1997), there has been a growing body of work that depicts living outside of the bounds of heterosexuality (see, for example, Green 2000; Green and Mitchell 2008; Greenan and Tunnel 2003; Laird 1999; Laird and Green 1996; LaSala 2007). In 2000, a special section of the *Journal of Marital and Family Therapy* was devoted to lesbian, gay, and bisexual issues in family therapy, and in 2006, an issue of the *Journal of Feminist Family Therapy* was devoted exclusively to lesbian families. Lev (2004) documented the gender revolution that was underway; her work upended essentialist notions of gender and expanded possibilities about what could be understood as "normal" and "healthy." Despite this forward movement, however, the literature and training in the field of family therapy is still primarily situated in the paradigm that privileges heterosexuality.

Fortunately, we can begin to imagine a more expansive view of relational health not linked exclusively to heterosexuality and traditional gender roles. For example, Knudson-Martin and Laughlin (2005) call for the development of new models of health and normalcy that are based on relational equality rather than gender. Stone-Fish and Harvey (2005) urge family therapists to attempt to develop family environments that actually nurture queerness.

Queering Family Therapy

Critiques from postmodern and queer theory challenge the construction of sexualities in general (Foucault 1981; Langdridge 2008; McPhail 2004; Seidman 1996; Warner 1993). They assert that by not challenging the gender binary, masculinity and femininity are reified and heterosexuality institutionalized. Queer theory suggests that the study of homosexuality should not be about the identity of a sexual minority group but rather about the need to question the social practices that "organize society as a whole by sexualizing—heterosexualizing or homosexualizing—bodies, desires, acts, identities, social relations, knowledges, cultures, [and] institutions" (Seidman 1996, pp. 12–13). According to Stone Fish and Harvey (2005), queer identity belongs to "anyone who violates the basic assumptions of heterosexuality" (p. 27). The field of family therapy has taken a stance of accommodating to or managing nonheterosexuality by helping families to "cope" with a LGBT member (Stone Fish and Harvey 2005). This approach is inherently pathologizing as it posits that any nonheterosexual or gender-variant family member is something to be "managed." By not questioning current language, false dichotomies, and essentialist views, family therapy colludes with the discourses that, at worst, pathologize the natural variability of human nature, and, at a minimum, render variations invisible. According to Perlesz and colleagues (2007), a lack of accepted and universally understood terms to describe nonheterosexual family relationships limits family narratives. The experiences of nonheterosexual parents are not included, invalidating both the parents' relationship and the family as a whole.

How would our language change if we embraced the belief that variation is the norm? What would this render possible when working with families? A true second-order change would not only embrace diversity as normative, but would also uphold the value and beauty of nonheterosexual or gender-variant family members not *in spite of* their identity but *because* of it. This would be family therapy transformed. This would actually be breaking down the heterosexual core of the idea of "family." How then might we understand what is unique about families created outside the bounds of heterosexuality, and as a result, bow would this inform our work with all families?

"Doing Family": Family Therapy Transformed

It is helpful to think about a shift in language that allows family to be considered as a verb, thus enabling us to "do family" (Stiles 2002). In the same way that Butler (1990) entertained the performative aspects of gender, "family" would be transformed to a more fluid, ambiguous entity that embraces diversity and variation as the norm. The performative aspect of "doing family" entails intentionally committing to add elements of responsibility and caretaking to the bonds of love, which usually embody roles traditionally assigned to kinship networks. Perlesz and colleagues (2006) point out that "doing family" is a counterpoint to the essentialist notions about "the family" as a discrete institution with particular boundaries. It creates possibilities for relating and parenting outside the bounds of heterosexual relationships.

In fact, because nonheterosexual couples and families are not limited to prescribed gender roles, their decisions about who does what in a relationship are often based on what each partner has skills in and/or enjoys, and are more likely to be egalitarian in household chores and childcare (Giammattei 2007; Green 2008; Patterson 1995). Some research suggests that lesbians tend to navigate older age with more resilience, possibly as a result of learning to deal with adversity (Gabbay and Wahler 2002). Children being raised by lesbian or gay couples are more likely to have two parents who are highly involved in their upbringing and care (Giammattei 2007; Patterson 2006). Lesbians and gay men have been found to be more satisfied with their relationships than heterosexual couples (Bigner 2000; McPherson 1993; Patterson 1995). It could also be argued that gay men who have been able to stay together in long, happy relationships while successfully navigating nonmonogamy may have something to teach others about surviving sexual encounters that occur outside the primary relationship (LaSala 2004). As the result of heteronormativity and a lack of openness to any divergence from the heterosexual ideal, these possible advantages are silenced and obscured, thereby making invisible factors that may actually help couples and families of all orientations and identities become more successful, satisfied, and happy.

Recently, researchers have begun to ask questions about what is unique or interesting about nonheterosexual families in and of themselves. In studying the ways in which women allocate work and parenting, Dunne (2000) found that the mothering experiences that lesbian women construct are qualitatively different from those in heterosexual coparenting. Mothering in a lesbian relationship is usually carried out in a context where both mothers receive a great deal of practical and emotional support from their partners, routine domestic responsibilities are shared, and there is a mutual recognition of a woman's right to an identity beyond the home. Without the prescriptive gender divisions of labor both within and outside of the home, these lesbian comothers have greater latitude to operationalize their egalitarian ideals, particularly in relation to parenting. Dunne states:

> In their everyday lives of nurturing, housework, and breadwinning, respondents provide viable alternative models for parenting beyond heterosexuality…. Their positioning outside conventionality and the similarities they share as women enable and indeed insist upon the redefinition of the meaning and content of motherhood. (p. 32)

Perlesz and colleagues (2007) found that lesbian-headed families often expand the notion of family by creating "families of choice," which might include both immediate and extended biological relatives and social and friendship networks. Thus if "family" is examined from the perspective provided by those who are finding new ways of "doing family," the opportunity will emerge to discover a more expansive way of relating while further deconstructing heteronormative ideas and practices. As Perlesz and colleagues explain,

> Thinking of ourselves and our clients as doing family opens up a greater repertoire for flexibility, negotiated meanings, fluidity, and ambiguity. It acknowledges, too, that families are in a social time of transition and flux. The families in our study show us that it is not always comfortable living differently. Understanding the tension that arises in attempting to do family within and beyond a heteronormative frame provides a useful starting point for tackling the everyday vicissitudes of family life that bring lesbian, gay, and straight families to therapy. (p. 197)

Shifting the Paradigm

We are only just beginning to understand the impact of heteronormative culture and the ways in which it has shaped conceptualizations of normalcy, health, and "legitimate" relationships. How can we begin to deconstruct family and disentangle it from the heteronormative paradigm?

Typically, instruction in family therapy includes the presentation of core theories (such as structural, strategic, solution focused) with some integration of the critiques emanating from feminist, postmodern, or social justice approaches. Even with these additional lenses, students of family therapy learn models that implicitly represent a particular kind of family structure: white, heterosexual, middle class, with "add on" components of ethnicity, gender, race, class, and sexual orientation in order to be more inclusive. In this approach, dominant cultural norms about family are the center from which theory and practice derive. One need only look at introductory family therapy texts to find evidence of this fact. The question we then raise is: How does the field move toward a paradigm that celebrates gender and sexual diversity as a norm? We offer some preliminary ideas.

Attend to the Use of Language and Name What Has Been Silenced

Both the presumption of heterosexuality and the essentialist and binary assumptions about masculinity and femininity can be made much more explicit in professional discourses. Students can be taught the importance of how language is used and the skill of noticing what goes unnamed. In this way, essentialist notions of gender and of heterosexuality can be removed from their current default positions. We attempt to consistently deconstruct binary notions of gender and do not presume that a "couple" or "family" is heterosexual. Together with students, we practice the simple but very powerful act of naming heterosexuality.

Understand the Impact of Heteronormative Culture on Research and Practice

Many of the past studies of gay and lesbian parents were shaped and constrained by a heteronormative lens. Since lesbian and gay parents were often denied custody of their children on the basis of sexual orientation, the research mandate was set to dispel common myths and assumptions held by most judges. Although maladjustment in children of heterosexual parents would not be an indictment of heterosexuality, the assumption was implicit that symptoms could be attributed to the "harmful" environment of LGBT lesbian and gay family life. It was thus necessary to establish that there was no difference between children raised by lesbian and gay parents when compared to those raised by heterosexual parents (Patterson 2006; Stacey and Biblarz 2001; Tasker and Patterson 2007).

This approach to the study of LGBT families has led to a "normalizing" discourse that has permeated the field. Children of gay and lesbian parents must look like children of heterosexual parents. Gay and lesbian families must be similar to heterosexual families. The discourses of "no difference" and "normalizing" are fundamentally defensive and apologetic. Yoshino (2006) described the mandate for all outsider groups to assimilate to the dominant norm as a "covering" demand, the expectation that how a person's identity is expressed should conform. For example, one can *be* gay or lesbian, but must still *look and act* according to the confines of heterosexual norms. According to Yoshino, "The contemporary resistance to gay marriage can be understood as a covering demand: *'Fine, be gay, but don't shove it in our faces'*" (p. 19). Covering, be believes, is the paramount civil rights issue of our time.

Another way to investigate the impact of heteronormativity is to utilize the concept of microaggressions—the brief, commonplace verbal, behavioral, and environmental indignities experienced by nonheterosexual families and other marginalized groups. These microaggressions can manifest in a variety of ways that are subtle and unintentional, and can include invisibility, silence, intrusive questioning, and the limitations of language to describe relationship and familial bonds. Developing a clear description of the incidence and impacts of microaggressions could do much to sensitize students to the negative cumulative effects of heteronormativity on LGBT families.

Include an Examination of Heterosexual Privilege

The privileges of a heterosexual lifestyle are vast and can operate in both an overt and covert fashion. For example, people of all sexual orientations have the right to talk about who they are without the necessity of discussing sexual behavior as the central component of their identity. The barrier that many heterosexual people describe as inhibiting their capacity for authentic intimate relationships with LGBT people is their assumption that sexuality will be central to conversation. Heterosexual youth are allowed to talk about their interests, beliefs, and relationships without discussing sexual behavior, whereas sexual minority youth do not hold this privilege.

Hudak (2007) points out that the heterosexual part of marriage remains largely detached from any analysis of relationship in the marriage and family therapy literature. This has obfuscated the fact that gender oppression can coexist with heterosexual privilege. Although women may experience gender oppression within the context of heterosexual marriage, they are simultaneously conferred significant social status and a variety of economic and legal rights and protections based on their partnerships with men. Incorporating heterosexual privilege into our analysis of relationship also would foster a deeper understanding of intersectionality. Those whose lives have been marginalized by their gender, race, and/or class often fail to recognize their heterosexual privilege and may resist the use of civil rights as a framework for discussing LGBT exclusion. Students could gain the capacity to support conversations that examine the various and complex forms of subjugation and privilege that exist simultaneously and function to shape the lives of families.

Conclusion

We are only beginning to understand the ways in which heteronormativity, the practices and institutions that legitimize and privilege heterosexuality, shape cultural conceptions of health and normalcy. Decentering heteronormativity is a generative process; it creates possibilities for being in the world and in relationship outside the confines of heterosexuality and traditional gender roles. It transforms the notion of "family" as a static entity to a verb that enables us to "do family." "Doing family" celebrates diversity and variation as the new norm, enhances research questions, and furthers scholarship and social justice.

To decenter heteronormativity, the rules of culture must be suspended—particularly the constraints attached to binary definitions of gender, family, and sexual orientation. Indeed, the very ways that Western thought is organized "around a series of dualities, of operations of comparing and contrasting" (Hare-Mustin 2004, p. 15) maintains the illusion of binaries—male/female, heterosexual/gay—always subjugating one to the other. To abandon these discourses would mean articulating a challenge to "traditional" family values.

What is the definition of a marriage or a family? Who gets to decide, and for what purpose? Will nonheterosexual couples and families be included in considering current definitions? As family therapists, we are uniquely poised to transform the meanings attached to "marriage" and "family"—to focus on the *quality* of relationship rather than on the gender of a partner or the assumption of particular roles. We have attempted to take a step forward in grappling with these questions, beginning what we hope is a long and fruitful conversation.

References

Allen, K. R., & Demo, D. H. (1995). The families of lesbian and gay men: A new frontier in family research. *Journal of Marital and Family Therapy, 57*, 1–17.

Bigner, J. (2000). Gay and lesbian families. In W. C. Nichols, M. A. Pace-Nichols, D. S. Becvar, & A. Y. Napier (Eds.), *Handbook of family development and intervention: Wiley series in couples and family dynamics and treatment* (pp. 279–298). New York, NY: John Wiley & Sons, Inc.

Bruner, J. (2002). *Making stories: Law, literature, life*. New York, NY: Farrar, Straus and Giroux.

Butler, J. (1990). *Gender trouble*. New York, NY: Routledge.

Clark, W. M., & Serovich, J. M. (1997). Twenty years and still in the dark? Content analysis of articles pertaining to gay, lesbian, and bisexual issues in marriage and family *therapy journals. Journal of Marital and Family Therapy, 23*, 239–253.

Diamond, L. M. (2008a). Female bisexuality from adolescence to adulthood: Results from a 10-year longitudinal study. *Developmental Psychology, 44*(1), 5–15.

Diamond, L. M. (2008b). Sexual fluidity: Understanding women's love and desire. Cambridge, MA: Harvard Press.

Dunne, G. (2000). Opting into motherhood: Lesbians blurring the boundaries and transforming the meaning of parenting and kinship. *Gender and Society, 14*, 11–35.

Fausto-Sterling, A. (2000). Of gender and genitals: The use and abuse of the modern inter-sexual. *Sexing the body: Gender politics and the construction* of *sexuality*. New York, NY: Basic Books.

Flax, J. (1990). Postmodern and gender relations in feminist theory. In L. Nicholson (Ed.), *Feminism/Postmodernism* (pp. 39–62). New York, NY: Routledge.

Foucault, M. (1981). *The history of sexuality, volume one: An introduction*. London, UK: Penguin.

Gabbay, S. G., & Wahler, J. J. (2002). Lesbian aging: Review of a growing literature. *Journal of Gay & Lesbian Social Services, 14*(3), 1–21.

Gamson, J. (2000). Sexualities, queer theory, and qualitative research. In N. Denzin & Y. Lincoln (Eds.), *Handbook of qualitative research* (2nd ed., pp. 347–365). Thousand Oaks, CA: Sage.

Giammattei, S. V. (2007). Family relations and emotional intelligence of children raised by lesbian or heterosexual parents. Unpublished doctoral dissertation. San Francisco, CA: Alliant University.

Green, R-J. (2000). Lesbians, gay men and their parents: A critique of LaSala and the prevailing clinical "wisdom." *Family Process, 39*, 257–266.

Green, R-J. (2008). What straights can learn from gays about relationships and parenting. *Quarterly Voice*, *7*(1), 11.

Green, R-J., & Mitchell, V. (2008). Gay and lesbian couples in therapy: Minority stress, relational ambiguity, and families of choice. In A. S. Gurman (Ed.), *Clinical handbook of couple therapy* (4th ed., pp. 662–680). New York, NY: Guilford Press.

Greenan, D. E., & Tunnel, G. (2003). *Couple therapy with gay men*. New York, NY: Guilford.

Harding, S. (1990). Feminism, science, and the anti-enlightenment critiques. In L. Nicholson (Ed.), *Feminism/postmodernism* (pp. 83–106). New York, NY: Routledge.

Hare-Mustin, R. T. (1994). Discourses in the mirrored room: A postmodern analysis of therapy. *Family Process*, *33*(l), 19–36.

Hare-Mustin, R. T. (2004). Can we demystify theory? Examining masculinity discourses and feminist postmodern theory. *Journal of Theoretical and Philosophical Psychology. 24*(1), 14–29.

Hudak, J. (2007). Are we not family? The transition from heterosexual marriage to partnering with a woman. Unpublished doctoral dissertation. Philadelphia, PA: Drexel University.

Knudson-Martin, C., & Laughlin, M. J. (2005). Gender and sexual orientation in family therapy: Toward a postgender approach. *Family Relations, 54*(1), 101–115.

Laird, J. (1999).Gender and sexuality in lesbian relationships. In J. Laird (Ed.), *Lesbians and lesbian families: Reflections on theory and practice* (pp. 47–90). New York, NY: Columbia University Press.

Laird, J. (2003). Lesbian and gay families. In F. Walsh (Ed.), *Normal family processes* (pp. 176–209). New York, NY: Guilford.

Laird, J., & Green, R-J., (Eds.) (1996). *Lesbians and gays in couples and family therapy: A handbook for therapists*. San Francisco, CA: Jossey-Bass.

Langdridge, D. (2008). Are you angry or are you heterosexual? A queer critique of lesbian and gay models of identity development. In L. Moon (Ed.) *Feeling queer or queer feelings? Radical approaches to counseling sex, sexualities and genders* (pp. 23–35). New York, NY: Routledge/ Taylor & Francis Group.

LaSala, M. C. (2004). Monogamy of the heart: Extradyadic sex and gay male couples. *Journal of Gay & Lesbian Social Services, 17*(3) 2–24.

LaSala, M. C. (2007). Old maps, new territory: Family therapy theory and gay and lesbian couples. *Journal of GLBT Family Studies, 3*(1), 1–14.

Lather, P. (1992).Postmodernism and the human sciences. In S. Kvale (Ed.), *Psychology and postmodernism* (p. 88–109). London, UK: Sage.

Lev, A. (2004).*Transgender emergence: Therapeutic guidelines for working with gender-variant people and their families*. New York, NY: Haworth Clinical Practice Press.
McPhail, B. A. (2004). Questioning gender and sexuality binaries: What queer theorists, transgendered individuals, and sex researchers can teach social work. *Journal of Gay & Lesbian Social Services, 17*(1), 3–21.
McPherson, D. (1993). Gay parenting couples: Parenting arrangements, arrangement satisfaction, and relationship satisfaction. Unpublished doctoral dissertation. Palo Alto, CA: Pacific Graduate School of Psychology.
Morris, A. (2006, February 6). Love and the ambisexual, heterofiexible teen. *New York*, 26–33.
Oswald, R. M., Blume, L. B., & Marks, S. R. (2005). Decentering heteronormativity: A model for family studies. In V. Bengston, A. Acock, K. Allen, P. Dilworth-Anderson, & D. Klein (Eds.), *Sourcebook of family theory and research* (pp. 143–165). Thousand Oaks, CA: Sage.
Patterson, C. J. (1995). Families of the baby boom: Parents' division of labor and children's adjustment. *Developmental Psychology, 31*, 115–123.
Patterson, C. (2006). Children of lesbian and gay parents. *Current Directions in Psychological Science, 15*(5), 241–244.
Perlesz, A., Brown, R., Lindsay, J., McNair, R., de Vaus, D., & Pitts, M. (2006). Family in transition: Parents, children and grandparents in lesbian families give meaning to "doing family." *Journal of Family Therapy, 28*(2), 175–199.
Savin-Williams, R. (2005). *The new gay teenager*. Cambridge, MA: Harvard University Press.
Sedgwick, E. K. (1990). *Epistemology of the closet*. Berkeley, CA: University of California Press.
Seidman, S. (1996). Introduction. In S. Seidman (Ed.), *Queer theory/sociology* (pp. 1–29). Cambridge, MA: Blackwell.
Spaulding, F. (1999). Unconsciousness-raising: Hidden dimensions of heterosexism in theory and practice with lesbians. In J. Laird (Ed.), *Lesbians and lesbian families: Reflections on theory and practice* (pp. 11–26). New York, NY: Columbia University Press.
Stacey, J., & Biblarz, T. J. (2001). (How) does the sexual orientation of the parents matter? *American Sociological Review, 66*(2), 159–183.
Stiles, S. (2002). Family as a verb. In D. Denborough (Ed.), *Queer Counseling and Narrative Practice* (pp. 15–19). Adelaide, SA: Dulwiche Center Publications.
Stone Fish, L., & Harvey, R. G. (2005). *Nurturing queer youth: Family therapy transformed*. New York, NY: W. W. Norton.
Tanner, L. R., & Lyness, K. P. (2003). Out of the closet, still in the home: Providing queer affirmative treatment for youth and their families. *Journal of Feminist Family Therapy, 15*(1), 21–35.
Tasker, F., & Patterson, C. J. (2007). Research on gay and lesbian parenting: Retrospect and prospect. *Journal of GLBT Family Studies, 3*(2/3), 9–34.
Warner, M. (1993). Introduction. In M. Warner (Ed.), *Fear of a queer planet: Queer politics and social theory* (pp. vii-xxxi). Minneapolis, MN: University of Minnesota Press.
Yoshino, K. (2006). *Covering: The hidden assault on our civil rights*. New York, NY: Random House.

Part VI
At the Edge: Exploring Gender and Sexuality in Couples and Families, 2011—Arlene Lev and Jean Malpas, Guest Editors

Families in Transition: Supporting Families of Transgender Youth

Melissa MacNish and Marissa Gold-Peifer

Gender is a core construct around which families explicitly and implicitly organize. As a result, the impact of a family member's expressing a desire to change gender presentation is not limited to the individual, but extends to the family system as well (Hill et al. 2010; Lev 2004). A shift in a family member's gender identity can have a wide-ranging impact on roles in the family, internal cognitive schemas, and family traditions and rituals.

According to the diagnostic manual (DSM-IV-TR; APA 2000) of the American Psychiatric Association (APA), Gender Identity Disorder (GID) has been the diagnosis[1] for individuals who exhibit behaviors consistent with cross-gender identification and who experience "discomfort with one's sex or gender role" (APA 2000, p. 871). The inclusion of GID in the DSM-IV stirred considerable controversy centering on a number of issues, one being that the diagnosis pathologizes gender "nonconformity" (Gainor et al. 2000; Hill et al. 2010; Lev 2005; Schwartz and Barber 2010; Spack 2009). The authors of this chapter do not view gender nonconformity as pathological. Clinical work with this population is approached as collaborative, helping guide families along their journey of self-exploration.

Gender "nonconforming" behavior may first be expressed and recognized by caretakers as early as 2 years old (Brill and Pepper 2008; Ehrensaft 2009; Pleak 2009; Vanderburgh 2008). However, this is not to say that all children who present this way in childhood will go on to identify as transgender later (Cohen-Kettenis and Pfafflin 2003; Ehrensaft 2009; Pleak 2009). While there is an emerging body of literature and awareness about the experience of being transgender, this topic

Editors' note: First published in 2011, American Family Therapy Academy Monograph Series.

[1] Editors' note: The 2013 edition of the DSM (DSM-V) reclassified GID as "Gender Identity Dysphoria," effectively downgrading it from a "disorder" to a "confusion."

M. MacNish (✉) · M. Gold-Peifer
Boston, MA, USA
e-mail: melissamacnishlmhc@gmail.com

T. Nelson, H. Winawer (eds.), *Critical Topics in Family Therapy*,
AFTA SpringerBriefs in Family Therapy, DOI 10.1007/978-3-319-03248-1_13,

remains vastly underrepresented in clinical training (Carroll and Gilroy 2002; Ehrbar et al. 2008; Gainor et al. 2000; Pleak 2009). This body of literature includes family adjustment stage models, as well as models of transgender identity development (Devor 2004; Emerson and Rosenfeld 1996; Lev 2004). Although each individual and family is unique, these stage models can provide a useful framework for understanding the experience of transgender individuals of different ages and their families (Saeger 2006). While the scope of this chapter does not allow for an exploration of the models, it is important for clinicians to be aware of them in working with this population.

Many families disconnect during the coming out process for gays, lesbians, bisexuals, and transgender individuals. Others are able to grow and even flourish from this experience, often in ways they did not consider possible (Gold 2008). This chapter explores how clinicians can foster connection in families. For purpose of this chapter, *youth* are defined as ages 15–23 as this is the age range of the people with whom the authors worked. Therapy with families whose children remain home and whose children have left home presents different challenges.

The term *transgender* will be used as an umbrella term for variations of gender identities that deviate from the expected gender presentation at birth and the roles families and society hold for those expectations. The term *transition* is used to mean any significant changes in gender expression causing turmoil in the family. This could range from a change in dress, the request to be called a different name, the use of different pronouns, and/or the desire for medical intervention such as hormone or surgical treatment.

This chapter is organized by a discussion of each theme derived from Gold's (2008) qualitative dissertation study, each followed by a discussion of clinical implications. As with any treatment, when a family presents with concerns surrounding their child's gender, the initial focus of treatment is assessment (Hill et al. 2010; Vanderburgh 2008). The family structure should be analyzed and other possible forms of psychopathology ruled out as primary explanations for gender differences or comorbid dysfunction (Israel and Tarver 1997).

Construction of Meaning

For some parents, a disclosure of transgender identity comes as a surprise; for others there has been an existing awareness that their child may be gay, lesbian, bisexual, or transgender. Parents frequently experience a sense of urgency to create a new understanding of their child's identity as well as their own as the family of a transgender person. This is fueled by the fact that youth have often engaged in internal processing of their gender identity for quite a while prior to disclosure and are further along in the process of transitioning. This gap, between the youth's and other family members' understanding, can increase the pressure to find a way of making sense of this experience and integrating the new information. Parents may be left feeling that their child is strides ahead of them in the process of making meaning and/or even in moving forward toward transition.

The way family members make meaning has an important impact on the adjustment process. One of the ways parents integrate their experience is by attempting to locate an etiology. Some of the information available on etiology of gender nonconformity points to parental pathology (Ehrensaft 2007; Emerson and Rosenfeld 1996). It is important that clinicians be aware of this and steer parents away from making meaning based on blame (Hill et al. 2010). Research on family resilience supports the notion that the assignment of blame to oneself or one's children can hinder adjustment to a stressor (Walsh 2003). When parents recognize that no one is to blame for the youth's gender identity, their abilities to cope and adjust are supported.

The authors of this chapter have often observed that caretakers make sense through the process of developing *narrative coherence,* the integration of past and present experiences in a way that allows for a sense of continuity (Beeler and DiProva 1999). In the experience of a family with a transgender youth, this integration develops as parents begin to see the youth's earlier behavior and/or distress in light of this new information. For many parents, this new information is helpful in the process of adjustment. Moreover, many youth show improvement in overall functioning and emotional well-being after disclosure and, for some, as they continue with a transition process (Ehrensaft 2009; Gold 2008). In many cases, the authors of this chapter have seen that individuals' increased levels of general functioning as they are allowed to express their gender identity more freely contributes to the parental acceptance.

Clinical Implications

When first working with families after the initial disclosure of a youth's transgender identity, it is crucial to set up agreements identifying how to keep the therapeutic space safe for all family members. These agreements are necessary because each family member will likely be at a different place in their acceptance/tolerance of this issue. The therapist must balance holding multiple alliances while always monitoring respectful communication between members. It is also important to assess each family's understanding of gender and gender stereotypes from their cultural perspective.

Therapists must have an understanding of the distinctions between biological sex, gender expression, gender identity, and sexual orientation (Ehrensaft 2009; Lev 2004). Psychoeducation and experiential exploration of the fluidity of these dimensions, as well as the fundamental differences between experiences of gender identity ("who one is") versus sexual orientation ("who one is physically attracted to"), is essential for clients, parents, and other family members. A useful intervention is to visually create the dimensions and encourage individuals to map themselves within each dimension according to their understanding of the term in general, their own positions, and the position of the transgender youth. The mapping may correspond to the present time, a time in the past, or a future time. This helps to experientially convey the fluidity among the dimensions and also across time.

While families are trying to make sense of this issue, there may be a discrepancy between members as to what people understand about gender and the transgender experience. Family members may find it helpful to research the topics outside of sessions. Therapists should assess family members' receptivity and provide appropriate resources (Vanderburgh 2008).

One intervention the authors of this chapter have found extremely useful for bridging the gap between a youth's understanding of his or her gender identity and the family's view is the *gender timeline.* First, without the family present, the youth is encouraged to make a timeline starting from birth to the present including any memories related to gender. Providing the youth with time to identify the first salient gender-related memory is often useful. From that point, the individual can be asked to construct a timeline on large paper according to the time increments he or she feels are meaningful. For example, some individuals have very early memories that have persisted across many years and find it most useful to break down the timeline year by year. For others, it may be more useful to break down the timeline according to developmental stages. This timeline can then be explored further with the therapist and, once the youth is comfortable, it can be presented to the family. This often provides the family with a better understanding of the progression of the youth's experience of his or her gender identity. The clinician can then invite the family to add their own memories, experiences, and questions, allowing for integration of a more cohesive collective family narrative. This collaborative intervention serves to enhance all family members' understanding of the gender narrative and may provide the youth with a sense of being more deeply understood.

Support

Research on family resilience consistently supports the idea that families who seek and obtain social support demonstrate greater resilience in the face of stressors (Simon et al. 2005). Adjustment to the disclosure of a transgender identity is no exception. Families who are able to reach out, locate, and make use of support systems frequently describe great relief in discovering others who are struggling with a similar experience (Gold 2008). Parents further describe how helpful it is to have their thoughts, feelings, and concerns normalized and validated.

This support and connection is especially important in relation to gender identity/expression because the stigma that surrounds gender variance in this culture can create a sense of isolation for family members. While there have been advances in recent years in the understanding and acceptance of variance from cultural gender norms, our society is still anchored in a dichotomous view of gender (Ehrensaft 2007). The stigma of being transgender often prevents individuals from seeking out and obtaining needed social support. Parents often describe their own dilemmas about how to "come out," worrying about to whom it is safe to disclose their child's identity. When local or face-to-face support is not available, social supports on the internet provide anonymity and allow for access to information and support from family members of transgender youth (Carroll and Gilroy 2002; Gold 2008).

Clinical Implications

Family therapy perspectives and systemic thinking are especially salient when working with families with transgender youth because a gender transition will have implications for many relationships within many systems in ways that are different from disclosure of other secrets. Families, and thus their friends, must relate to the transgender person in a much different way. Helping the family to create a visual diagram of representative circles (sometimes called a sociogram) with the family at the center and different extended communities (extended family members, friends, work, school, religious communities, etc.) with which they interact helps the family assess support and guide planful disclosures within those systems (cf. Imber-Black 1998 for ideas on helping families disclose secrets in general). This intervention with the family assists conceptualization of the people in their lives to whom and when disclosure is necessary.

An initial task for the family is to identify those supports they predict may be more understanding and begin disclosure with them. Role playing with clients and working collaboratively around the disclosure process can help reduce the fear and anxiety associated with disclosing secrets, and also provides an opportunity to strengthen the family as they discuss relationships and actions together.

When family members feel more comfortable about the youth's gender identity, disclosures will proceed more smoothly. Families must consider the multiple systems within which their lives intersect such as neighborhood, community, school system, and religious community when making determinations about disclosure. For example, navigating school systems can be quite difficult for adolescents and their parents (Hill et al. 2010; Pleak 2009). Unfortunately, it is common for transgender youth to encounter stigma, including harassment in school (Toomey et al. 2010). Families should be prepared for negative and even hostile reactions (Vanderburgh 2008). One concrete way to prepare for adverse reactions is by the creation of a "safe folder" as suggested by Trans Youth Family Allies (TYFA 2010). A safe folder consists of documents from individuals such as healthcare providers, family friends, or religious leaders that detail and support the youth's gender identity and the family's stability.

Clinicians working with this population should become familiar with safe spaces in the community such as support groups or drop-in centers and refer families and youth when appropriate. These safe spaces can be especially important given the stigma around gender variation (Stone Fish and Harvey 2005). Support groups for parents, whether virtual or in person, can offer needed connection where parents do not have to censor their feelings from their child. PFLAG (Parents, Families, and Friends of Lesbians and Gays) meetings serve this purpose for some families.

Because there are unique issues in having a trans-gender child that differ from a child's disclosing an alternative sexual orientation, it became clear to the authors of this chapter that there was a need for a support group specific for parents with adolescent/young adult children who identified as transgender in the Boston area. The authors partnered with Greater Boston PFLAG and the Sidney Borum Junior Health Center to start such a group. This group has been in existence for over 2 years and it keeps growing to include more parents of younger and older children alike. It is amazing to witness parents who are struggling come into a group for the first time and meet other parents who are further along in the process of acceptance. These parents offer support and hope, and form strong connections, while modeling a path to regaining stability and normalcy.

The authors of this chapter also have witnessed the power of a supportive environment for transgender and gender nonconforming youth and their families through serving on the board of directors and acting as parent liaisons for Camp Aranu'tiq[2], a week-long summer camp for transgender/gender nonconforming youth ages 8–15. The camp's inaugural summer in 2010 highlighted the profound value even a week of support and acceptance can have for youth and their families. Many of the youth described feeling safe, understood, and proud of who they are for the first time in their lives. The authors observed and others reported improvements in self-esteem, family acceptance, and peer relationships. The campers were also able to discover other aspects of themselves, and were able to explore and exercise their capacities for leadership.

This camp provided parents an opportunity to meet as a group when they dropped their children off. Parents and caretakers from all different parts of the country were present, and for some it was their first opportunity to meet other parents of transgender youth. Watching these family members nod their heads in understanding and relief that they had found others in similar situations was extremely powerful to witness. However, the most profound moments were when parents and caretakers reunited with their children after the children had been allowed to have a week to be their authentic selves. Watching the reactions of amazement that their children fit in, made friends, and, in some cases, even performed in the talent show, solidified for us the power of a supportive environment. Many of these families and youth have remained in contact and continue to support each other.

Flexibility and Stability

A balance between flexibility and stability is often demonstrated by families who are moving toward acceptance of their children's transgender identity. Flexibility is critical for family coping as it enhances the family's ability to more readily develop

[2] For more information on this camp see www.camparanutiq.org.

a new sense of normalcy (Patterson 2002). Flexibility within a family facilitates movement toward a new homeostasis after the disclosure and throughout the transition process. Although flexibility and the capacity for change are critically important, it is equally important that flexibility be balanced with consistency and stability. Those families that have been able to adjust more readily to their adolescents' gender identity often report that they have established family routines, traditions, and rituals that have continued in the face of the family stressor. At times, families may need to rework routines, traditions, or rituals according to the new information about their child's gender identity. Continued stability often provides a sense of safety for the family and serves as a foundation from which the family is able to engage in the work necessary to adjust to this experience.

Similar to the need for balance between flexibility and consistency is the need for balance between cohesion and individuality within the family unit. The literature on family resilience and coping suggests that it is important for family members to allow space for a range of emotions in dealing with a crisis (Walsh 2003). This is evident in the responses of parents in Gold's (2008) study and in the clinical experience of the authors of this chapter. Many parents talk about the need for and value of having a space where they feel permission to express a range of emotions. Parents who are partnered speak of the importance of allowing their partners to be in a different place in their process of acceptance. Conflict often results when there is not an understanding that family members may experience different feelings at different times and in different ways.

Clinical Implications

Most importantly, therapists who work with transgender youth and their families must be flexible in their thinking in practice and their professional roles. For example, clinicians may take on the role of advocate for the families and youth with whom they work. Clinicians may become advocates for transgender individuals within schools, communities, and even political systems, yet must balance this with helping youth and families to advocate for themselves.

Clinicians working with families and transgender youth must also be flexible in their consideration and implementation of interventions. One example of a powerful, yet nontraditional, intervention is to connect clients with other families of transgender youth after receiving permission from all parties (Vanderburgh 2008). This can be especially helpful to those families experiencing isolation. In addition, putting families in touch with transgender mentors they trust in the community may be useful. Seeing transgender adults who are living rich and authentic lives can help families envision the possibility of normalcy.

Clinical attention should be paid to how a change in gender identity and gender roles will affect the family system and relationships within the family (Cooper 2009). Creating space for the exploration of these different and changing relationships is important. One useful intervention involves working with different subgroups in the family in order to strengthen those relationships that are experiencing greater difficulty. Some but not all existing conflicts between parents, siblings, or other family subgroups may be explored in the presence of the transgender youth. Meeting with individual family members to assess their unique experiences is another important intervention (LaSala 2010).

Although a family may need to change in many ways following the disclosure of transgender identity, it also is important that at least some family traditions or rituals continue in order to provide a greater sense of homeostasis and stability during the adjustment period (Gold 2008). Clinicians are encouraged to inquire about past and present family traditions or rituals, and to help create them when they have not been central to family life. Family therapy provides an instrumental forum to think through and renegotiate any family rituals or traditions that are specific to gender. Examples of family rituals that may be related to gender range from daily tasks such as meal preparation and yard work to annual family traditions such as male-only basketball games before holiday meals. Clinicians can provide "homework" assignments to help upset and realign these rituals. Although traditions and rituals aim to create a sense of belonging, they may lead to a sense of alienation if not renegotiated sensitively and carefully, including those traditions with extended family members. Helping a family to identify, create, renegotiate, or reengage in ritual and tradition will help provide a sense of stability as families adjust following disclosure.

Sensitive Communication

There is a unique challenge inherent in communication around changes in gender identity. Often, parents and family members are faced with adjusting their use of pronouns and names, and use of terms such as son/daughter and brother/sister. A change in the youth's name can be particularly difficult for parents, especially if the birth name was chosen because it had special meaning. The change in language is often an emotional one and requires a significant cognitive shift that takes effort and time to achieve. Families who are more readily able to adjust to this experience and maintain connection often describe the considerable effort they made, and continue to exert to use language consistent with the youth's preferred pronoun and name. The authors have witnessed that it is often very helpful for parents to identify the difficulty and to anticipate the inevitable mistakes they will make when it comes to language around gender. It is also important that youth be allowed and encouraged to articulate how it can be painful and/or embarrassing when a parent misuses a pronoun or given name. For example, a youth's transgender identity may be inadvertently disclosed by parents if they use "son" or "daughter" incorrectly in a social situation. A great deal of respect and support is conveyed to youth when parents and family members demonstrate sensitivity to communication and language.

Sensitive communication has a bidirectional impact on the family adjustment process. The youth's sensitive communication is particularly important during the disclosure process. Related research on the disclosure of gay, lesbian, and bisexual orientation suggests that the response to the disclosure can be mediated by the manner in which it is disclosed (Beeler and DiProva 1999; LaSala 2010). For example, finding out about an adolescent's sexual orientation by unexpectedly seeing him or her with a same-sex partner may be received more negatively than a youth's coming out in a more planned and verbal way. The authors of this chapter have found this is similar for the disclosure of a transgender identity. Especially for families who have not had a pre-existing awareness of their child's gender difference, sensitivity about communication on behalf of the youth when disclosing to their parents can be an initial step in the ability of families to adjust in a more resilient way. It also demonstrates maturity on the part of the youth.

Clinical Implications

Given the importance of sensitive communication in the adjustment process, assessing how youth disclosed their identities to each member of the family is often useful. Understanding more about the disclosures and family members' responses may provide valuable information on future family interactions. Feelings about how the disclosure was made may need to be processed further.

The therapeutic space often serves as a place for family members to explore implications of language and to practice using new language without judgment. Probably one of the greatest challenges for therapists is holding sensitive communication within the space. Making agreements at the beginning of therapy for how to keep the space safe reinforces respect for everyone. It should also be made explicit that there will likely be mistakes given the difficulty inherent in changing language. The more each family member is able to practice, especially in the safety of the therapy space, the more comfortable the family will feel, and the youth will feel increasingly seen.

Conclusion

This chapter explored four themes—constructing meaning, support, flexibility and stability, and sensitive communication—related to the family adjustment process following a youth's disclosure of transgender identity. The authors have found these themes to be helpful guides in clinical work with families of transgender youth after initial disclosure and throughout family therapy. Clinical implications pertaining to each theme were also provided.

Parents have conveyed that the process of adjustment is indeed a process that takes time. Consistent with stage models, acceptance of the transgender identity does not mean that there are no remaining areas of difficulty, rather that there has been movement away from isolation and shame toward integration of the adolescent's identity into the family and broader family community (Lev 2004). Families are able to move to a place of acceptance and even become activists for change in their community. This is captured by Brill and Pepper (2008) in the following statement: "There is a natural overflow into your daily life when you realize that there is nothing wrong with your child. If the problem lies with the system, then you work to change the system that discriminates against your child" (p. 59). Many families, some of whom even doubted their ability to ever accept their children's transgender identities, are now combating discrimination and fighting for the rights of their youth and all transgender individuals.

Acknowledgements We are grateful to the Sidney Borum Jr. Health Center, Fenway Health, JRI Health, Greater Boston Family Therapy Training Boston, and Camp Aranu'tiq for supporting our work with transgender youth and their families. Their support and guidance has been instrumental in our learning and clinical work with this complex family issue. It has been a particular honor and privilege to learn from the parents of the support group and to bear witness to all they have shared. We would also like to thank Thorana Nelson for her invaluable guidance through this writing process.

References

American Psychiatric Association. (2000). *Diagnostic and statistical manual of mental disorders* (4th ed., Text Revision). Washington, DC: Author.

Beeler, J., & Diprova, V. (1999). Family adjustment following disclosure of homosexuality by a member: Themes discerned in narrative accounts. *Journal of Marital and Family Therapy, 25*, 443–459.

Brill, S., & Pepper, R. (2008). *The transgender child: A handbook for families and professionals.* San Francisco, CA: Cleis Press.

Carroll, L., & Gilroy, P. J. (2002). Transgender issues in counselor preparation. *Counselor Education and Supervision, 41*(3), 233–242.

Cohen-Kettenis, P., & Pfafflin, F. (2003). *Transgenderism and intersexuality in childhood and adolescence: Making choices*. Thousand Oaks, CA: Sage.

Cooper, K. (2009). Social work practice with transgender and gender variant youth and their families. In G. P. Mallon (Ed.), *Social Work Practice with Transgender and Gender-variant Youth* (2nd ed.). New York, NY: Routledge.

Devor, A. (2004). Witnessing and mirroring: A fourteen stage model of transsexual identity formation. *Journal of Gay & Lesbian Psychotherapy, 8*, 41–67.

Ehrbar, R., Witty, M., Ehrbar, H., & Bockting, W. (2008). Clinician judgment in the diagnosis of gender identity disorder in children. *Journal of Sex & Marital Therapy, 34*(5), 385–412.

Ehrensaft, D. (2007). Raising girly boys: A parent's perspective. *Studies in Gender and Sexuality, 8*(3), 269–302.

Ehrensaft, D. (2009). One pill makes you boy, one pill makes you girl. *International Journal of Applied Psychoanalytic Studies, 6*(1), 12–24.

Emerson, S., & Rosenfeld, C. (1996). Stages of adjustment in family members of transgender individuals. *Journal of Family Psychotherapy, 7*(3), 1–12.

Gainor, K. A., Greene, B., & Croom, G. L. (2000). *Including transgender issues in lesbian, gay, and bisexual psychology: Implications for clinical practice and training.* Thousand Oaks, CA: Sage.

Gold, M. (2008). A qualitative Investigation into the process of family adjustment to transgender emergence. *Dissertation Abstract International, 69*(7), 135A.

Hill, D., Menvielle, E., Sica, K., & Johnson, A. (2010). An affirmative intervention for families with gender-variant children: Parental ratings of child mental health and gender. *Journal of Sex and Marital Therapy*, *36*(1), 6–23.

Imber-Black, E. (1998). *The secret life of families*. New York, NY: Bantam.

Israel, G. E., & Tarver, D. E. (Eds.) (1997). *Trans-gender care: Recommended guidelines, practical information, and personal accounts*. Philadelphia, PA: Temple University Press.

LaSala, M. C. (2010). *Coming out, coming home: Helping families adjust to gay or lesbian child*. New York, NY: Columbia University Press.

Lev, A. I. (2004). *Transgender emergence: Therapeutic guidelines for working with gender-variant people and their families*. New York, NY: Routledge.

Lev, A. I. (2005). Disordering gender identity: Gender identity disorder in the DSM-IV-TR. *Journal of Psychology & Human Sexuality*, *17*(3/4), 35–69.

Patterson, J. M. (2002). Understanding family resilience. *Journal of Clinical Psychology*, *58*(3), 233–246.

Pleak, R. (2009). Formation of transgender identities in adolescence. *Journal of Gay & Lesbian Mental Health*, *13*(4), 282–291.

Saeger, K. (2006). Finding our way: Guiding a young transgender child. *The Journal of GLBT Family Studies*, *2*(3/4), 207–245.

Schwartz, A., & Barber, M. (2010). An inside look: Appreciating the complexity of gender identity. *Journal of Gay & Lesbian Mental Health*, *14*(2), 91–93.

Simon, J. B., Murphy, J. J., & Smith, S. M. (2005). Understanding and fostering family resilience. *The Family Journal, 13(4)*, 427–436.

Spack, N. (2009). An endocrine perspective on the care of transgender adolescents. *Journal of Gay & Lesbian Mental Health*, *13*(4), 309–319.

Stone Fish, L., & Harvey, R. G. (2005). *Nurturing queer youth: Family therapy transformed*. New York, NY: W.W. Norton.

Toomey, R., Ryan, C., Diaz, R. M., Card, N. A., & Russell, S. T. (2010). Gender-nonconforming lesbian, gay, bisexual, and transgender youth: School victimization and young adult psychosocial adjustment. *Developmental Psychology*, *46*, 1580–1589.

Trans Youth Family Allies. (2010). Assembling a "Safe" Folder. Available at http://www.imatyfa.org/resources/parents/creating-a-safe-folder/

Vanderburgh, R. (2008). Appropriate therapeutic care for families with pre-pubescent transgender/gender-dissonant children. *Child and Adolescent Social Work Journal*, *26*(2), 135–154.

Walsh, F. (2003). Family resilience: A framework for clinical practice. *Family Process*, *42*(1), 1–18.

Erotic Fantasy Reconsidered: From Tragedy to Triumph

Esther Perel

> *A fantasy is a map of desire, mastery, escape, and obscuration; the navigational path we invent to steer ourselves between the reefs and shoals of anxiety, guilt, and inhibition. It is a work of consciousness, but in reaction to unconscious pressures. What is fascinating is not only how bizarre fantasies are, but how comprehensible; each one gives us a coherent and consistent picture of personality—the unconscious—of the person who invented it, even though he may think it the random whim of the moment.*
>
> Nancy Friday (1992)

Sexual fantasies are a wellspring of information about the individual's internal life and the relational dynamics of the couple. They remind us that sex isn't something we do, but a place we go, inside ourselves and with another. Too often, couples focus almost exclusively on the act and the statistics of sex, especially if they are caught in a sexual stalemate. "Three times a week is too much, but twice, is too little." "We both have orgasms, but sex is always the same… the whole thing lasts 10 min from beginning to end." "Conditions are never right, I can't remember the last time we had sex." The therapeutic approach described herein helps couples exit the "doing" story of sex, and enter their subjective and inter-subjective experience.

The erotic landscape is vastly larger, richer, and more intricate than any repertoire of sexual techniques. Sex is a receptacle for our longings, hopes, fears and struggles, and we invest our erotic encounters with a complex set of needs and expectations. We seek love, pleasure, escape, validation, ecstasy, to be seen, and even spiritual union.

Editors' note: First published in 2005, American Family Therapy Academy Monograph Series.

E. Perel (✉)
Family Studies Unit of the Department of Psychiatry, New York University Medical Center, New York, NY, USA

International Trauma Studies Program, Ackerman Institute for the Family, New York, NY, USA
e-mail: estherperel@me.com

T. Nelson, H. Winawer (eds.), *Critical Topics in Family Therapy*,
AFTA SpringerBriefs in Family Therapy, DOI 10.1007/978-3-319-03248-1_14,

In therapy, the role of sex in the couple's life is explored*: What does sex mean for you? What do you seek in sex? What do you want to experience in your encounters?* A wide range of feelings and desires can be heard in answers such as, "A longing-for communion and transcendence." "An expression of pure love." "The delightful feeling of being wanted, taken, ravished." "The wish to be taken care off without having to earn it." "The exuberance of release." "A safe place to experience aggression, power, and control, or the pleasure of losing control and surrender." "The melting of bodies which unleashes a unique kind of vulnerability and intimacy." "The permission to relinquish responsibility and to step out of one's familiar roles." "An act of rebellion against social conventions and the excitement of toppling the rules of good citizenship." "The experience of freedom, playfulness, naughtiness and transgression." "The trespassing of taboos." "A temporary merging, being simultaneously in and out of one's body, inside oneself and inside another." Or simply as one partner said, "To feel good."

Our emotional history shapes our erotic blueprint and is expressed in the physicality of sex. Accordingly, there is a strong connection between our attachment map—defined as our expectations, conflicts, hopes, and disillusionment with intimate connections—and our sexual feelings and behaviors: Tell me how you were loved, and I'll tell you how you make love. Were our parents or caregivers responsive to our needs or were we expected to monitor theirs? Did we turn to them for protection or did we flee to protect ourselves? Was pleasure celebrated, suspiciously tolerated, or simply dismissed? Did we feel safe to trust? Were we rejected? Humiliated? Abandoned? Were we held? Rocked? Soothed? Did we learn to receive or to be denied; to dare or to be afraid? Did we figure out not to expect too much and to hide when we were upset? In our family, we sense when it's okay to thrive and when others might be hurt by our zest. We learn how to feel about our body, our gender and our sexuality. And we learn a multitude of other lessons about whom to be and how to act that seep straight into our erotic life. All these experiences shape our beliefs about ourselves and our expectations from others. They are part of the dowry each man and woman brings to the unknown continent of adult love. Part of this emotional scorecard is obvious, but much of it is unspoken, concealed even from ourselves.

Upon careful listening to clients' erotic revelations, it becomes clear that fantasies are an imaginary transposition of their emotional needs into the creation of a paradigmatic erotic schema. A valuable creative resource, fantasies transform our emotional and existential quests into sources of pleasure. They offer us an imaginary pathway to repair, compensate, and transform. A couple is a gathering place where we bring these imaginary elaborations to bear. There is a dialectical relation between the power and dominance, the surrender, the dependency, and the care that we toy with in our sexual fantasies and the reality of a couple's life. The same power imbalance we fight about in the kitchen may incite our sexual excitement after dinner. It is, however, beyond the scope of this article to delve into the tensions and inconsistencies of power dynamics in couples and the intersections with sex.

One patient Joanna, a 51 year-old lab technician, has always approached the inner workings of her erotic mind with great trepidation. "Something would creep in and it would be dismissed before it could ever develop," she says. "You know, my fairy tale fantasy has always been, 'Oh, why don't we just cuddle? Wouldn't it be nice to just, like, rub my back?' But I realized my fantasy was very different."

She describes herself as a child living in the background of her family, often feeling invisible. She tells the story of how one night she woke up vomiting in her bed, afraid to call her parents for fear that it would disturb them and that they wouldn't take her seriously. She left a crumb on the side of her mouth, hoping that someone would notice her distress in the morning. They didn't.

The theme of invisibility looms large in the making of her erotic blueprint. It is dominated by the words, "I have enough, I don't need any more." The intricacies of our desire often lie buried in the details of our childhood. Our sexual proclivities arise from the thrills, challenges, and conflicts of our early life.

Joanna tells me that she has a deep wish for people to see her. "I want them to notice me, to watch me, to admire me, to *know* me." "Is this wish realized in your fantasies?" I ask. She tells me that she likes to be blindfolded and tied up. "In my fantasies, it's all about me. I don't have to do anything." I try to decipher the meaning of sexual fantasies by approaching them more as dreams or complex symbolic structures than as literal narratives of secret intentions. What happens in the fantasy of "tie me up" that meets that need?

Joanna explains: "When I am tied up, I don't have to think, I don't have to give or be nice. I cannot *not* let you give to me and I can't give anything because I'm tied up."

Recognizing the depth, complexity, and healing qualities of the erotic imagination, we explore sexual fantasy as a staging ground for action and escape that turns the tables on those responsible for earlier experiences of demoralization, defeat, and even trauma.

For Joanna, the restraint is not about force or being over powered. Rather it bypasses the ways that she stops herself from receiving pleasure, a lifelong habit of self-abnegation and disappearing in the background. When she is tied up she can only be given to, she needs not worry and feel guilty that she's taking too much, and she feels no pressure to instantly return the favor. In her fantasy, she is put in a situation where she has no other choice but to receive, legitimately and abundantly.

Understanding what fantasies do for our clients helps therapists to understand the emotional needs they bring to their sexual encounters. A good fantasy states the problem and offers the solution. It is an ingenious way for our creative mind to overcome all sorts of relational and intrapsychic conflicts around desire and intimacy. Psychoanalyst Michael Bader (2002), whose brilliant book *Arousal* offers an in-depth discussion of the undercurrents of fantasy, explains that in the sanctuary of the erotic mind we find a psychological safe space to undo the fears, inhibitions, and prohibitions that roil within us. Joanna frees herself from her psychological constraints and the limits put upon her by her conscience and her self-image. The ability to go anywhere in our imagination is a pure expression of individual freedom. It is a creative force that can help us momentarily transcend reality. In the playful twist of her erotic imagination, being entrapped unleashes her freedom.

Sex therapist Jack Morin (1995) explains that the erotic imagination is inventive in undoing, transforming, and redressing the traumas of the past. The very experiences that caused us the most pain in childhood sometimes become the greatest sources of pleasure and excitement later on.

Joanna's husband, Carl, recounts one of his formative memories: One evening as he sat next to his mother on the sofa watching TV, he unexpectedly brushed his leg against her skin and instantly recoiled in fear, a powerful blend of terror and longing. The tenderness he craved was a transgression into dangerous territory. This incident became a seminal experience in the shaping of his erotic blueprint. Carl's mother spent much time on the sofa smoking cigarettes and watching soap operas on television and he learned to hide his vulnerabilities and need for tender connection.

During the day, Carl was an engineer in charge of an entire division. After hours, his libidinal pursuits went into overdrive with on-line porn or off-line revelries, all depicting older women and young men/boys. In his imaginary world, the adult Carl could experience the needs the little boy had to repress—tenderness, softness, vulnerability, and dependency. All these repudiated emotions fueled his erotic scripts. There, Carl the man can play the little boy without suffering the pain of the little boy who was refused the soothing, loving touch of mother. In his fantasies he is not needy: the women always want him, they never say no, they know exactly what he needs, and are happy to give it to him. Reliving the little boy is frightening; to play him is enchanting. Fantasies express truths about ourselves that are hard to.get at otherwise. They reveal us at our most bare and in their own mysterious way they convey our deepest wishes.

Unfortunately, Carl's metaphors got confused. Need and desire got mixed up. Joanna is clear about that. "I don't mind nurturing the little boy, but I don't want to have sex with the little boy." She sees him as demanding; he sees her as withholding. She wishes he would desire her, he says why don't you want me? And both are saying, "See me, hear me, touch me, feel me."

Delving into narratives of fantasies, de-pathologizing them, translating the metaphors and the power of the turn-ons, connecting them to the person's emotional history, and then creating a bridge between past and present, self and other, are important steps in the therapeutic process. While for some, sharing fantasies is relationally intimate (the exposure of a unique nudity to one's partner), others would rather maintain an intimacy with themselves and prefer to host their revelries privately. This paper does not do justice to the intricacies and dilemmas of fantasy disclosure: Whether to tell? When? How? What for? Whether to enact them, and if so, how far? This paper discusses how we can use fantasies in therapy as a metaphoric language to address sexual impasses in the individuals and in the couple. Narrating our fantasies is an exercise in self-description, which in turn promotes differentiation between partners; it elicits separateness and curiosity, which is at once alluring and threatening. To turn the spotlight on oneself and to invite the other into a vulnerable territory puts responsibility on each person to own whom they are. It is the other side of blame. It involves not only trusting the other, but also the belief that one is worth being known, loved, and desired.

When clients open the door to their imaginary musings, offering literal translations can be tempting. Yet, any element of a fantasy—any object, toy, type of light, time of day, smell, or smile—has a subjective meaning that only the author of the plot stands to interpret.

One day, Joanna planned a sexual encounter. She put a note on the door that read "Help me!" and then she tied herself to the bed. When Carl arrived she sensed his hesitation, but she stayed focused on herself and did not worry about him. Her desire wasn't contingent on him; it was about her.

As a child, Joanna would leave minor marks on her body, like the crumb mentioned previously, hoping to be noticed. She was accustomed to receiving little response from her parents and had learned to protect herself from disappointment by leaving signs that were so subtle that if nobody noticed them, she could easily pretend they never existed. We named this the "crumb approach." For many years she would initiate sex with Carl using the same subterfuge. She would come on to him in a vague and non-committal manner so that when he refused her advances, it was barely evident she had ever taken initiative.

That day, she didn't just leave a crumb on her lip; she put herself in full view. There was nothing sheepish or tentative about her seduction. Not surprisingly, Joanna reveals that this was the first time in decades that she had an orgasm with Carl. She describes how she felt alive. We agree that the energy comes from her sense of self-worth and healthy entitlement that drive her action. Joanna was in the realm of desire, of owning the wanting. The script is sexual, but the risks she takes and the healing she experiences are quintessentially emotional. The pleasure is commensurate with the meaning far beyond its specific theatricality.

Reflecting on her boldness, Joanna tells me that in the past she would immediately whisk away any sexual thought she had. As she has become more comfortable with her thoughts, more open and connected to her sexuality, she meets herself anew. "I realized that I wanted to be dominated. I wanted him to be rough, which was so far away from where I ever thought or even dreamed that I would be. I didn't want to be hurt, though. I was very aggressive, very forthcoming with my wants. "I would like you to tie me up. I would like you to blindfold me. I don't want to know what you're going to do until you do it." Like that. And it was good. She said, "Oh my God, this is what it feels like to be alive."

When I inquired if she had feared Carl's reaction, she smiled and showed me with her hand how she had blindfolded herself. Some people may be very scared to place themselves in such an explicitly helpless state, but for Joanna, being unable to see freed her from self-consciousness, inhibition, and worry about Carl's reaction. Her disempowerment was a staged, assertive, and playful way to get Carl's attention, and he could, in turn, sidestep the allusions to the depressed mother on the couch. This time, he was able to respond to his wife with erotic fervor and desire. It was clear that he didn't need her. He wanted her.

Clearly, fantasies are not experiences we necessarily want to live in reality. When we act them out, we are playing, and when we play, we are in pretend mode, we are in control, especially if we decide not to be. To play we need to be free; to be free we need to feel safe. We don't play jail when we live in one. Fantasies are subversive, creative acts. Perhaps sex is never just sex?

Early childhood experiences of touch, play, or trauma become the cornerstone of our adult erotic life. In fact, one facet of the erotic blueprint that highlights the irrationality of our desire is that what excites us most will often arise from our childhood hurts and frustrations. Carl knew what he liked, but he had no idea what was so powerful about it. He had always sexualized his needs but he hadn't connected the dots. Growing up, he learned to live on a diet of quick pecks on the cheek from his mother to satisfy his emotional needs. Sex was the place where he lodged his need for security, for caring and communion. It was a perfect storage place for his suppressed emotional needs. When he felt rejected, his reactions could be extreme. For people like Carl, sexual frustration is physical and the emotional price they pay can feel unbearable. For them, sex is a lifeline through which they nurture their need for giving and receiving affection, love, care, tenderness, and for attunement. It is also a venue where they can be assertive, demanding, greedy, or needful, where they express themselves authentically and communicate in their most intimate voices. After all, it isn't only sex Carl is being denied, it's an entire emotional landscape that becomes sealed off.

I ask him if he ever puts his hands on Joanna's face. He doesn't. On her arm, yes; so, too, on her shoulder and her leg, but never her face. The face is the most vulnerable place to receive touch. When we hold someone's face in our hands or vice versa, it creates an inescapable focus between two people, a reminder of the primal parent—child gaze. Till now, Carl has only known motherly care and tender touch visually on a computer monitor screen. So I created an enactment in which he could experience some of his emotional needs in a non-sexual way and with a real live woman: his wife. The therapeutic intervention was to have Joanna hold his face so he could have a safe embodied encounter being gently held. At the start, Carl felt nauseated; he said he had a knot in his stomach. Once again his proclivity to physicalize feelings is at work here. It is palpable in his body. As the exercise progresses, slowly and carefully, Carl the adult will receive what the boy never did, clearing the way for the boy to grow into a man.

Similar to hypnotic induction, Carl is guided to take in the experience. I tell him, "As this new relatedness grafts itself under your skin, let it travel through you, through your nose and into the extremities of your fingers. As you take in her contact, you will breathe through the knot in your stomach, and at some point you will surrender to the embrace. From there you will reach for her face, but not by hunting for her; rather, you will reach her from within yourself."

This enactment took quite some time. While Carl soaked up the connection, I gently pressed him to nestle on Joanna, a sign of how far back he had to go and start from infancy onward. From a place of receiving, he slowly began to give. He held Joanna, her body, her face, his hands caressing. When he finally disentangled himself, he seemed to have come back from afar. He said, "I don't feel sick anymore. When I started, I felt really small, scared. Then I saw myself getting younger. I felt like a baby. I never experienced anything like that. I didn't know what to expect. I felt small, safe, loved, and then I started feeling myself getting a little older and bigger. And it still felt good, but in different way. And then it felt like wanting to give. Like an expression. It felt like it was just a part of me. It felt legitimate. And I wasn't punished. Nothing bad happened. It's a good feeling, to get this in real life, in real flesh."

In the past, Carl would often approach Joanna pretending to say: "I want you," but really saying, "Do you want me?" even demanding, "Want me!" His focus was on receiving. But he needed to add the dimension of giving. This is not something strange and new for him. Their relationship is infused with generosity, but not their sex life. It is the sexualizing of these obfuscated needs that makes all this so blurry.

In sex, he has to shift from needing the mother to wanting a woman; that is, to differentiate the motherly touch from the woman's sexual response. Then, Joanna can feel wanted instead of needed, and they will mark the first step out of their erotic ambush. The point is not at all to eradicate need or dependency; Carl and Joanna depend on each other for so much. Their relationship offers them a sense of grounding and anchoring, a feeling of belonging and continuity. This mutuality and reciprocity has made their 26 year-long marriage remarkably resilient. They have relied on each other to build a home, raise children, bury parents, acquire an education, change careers, discuss their personal challenges, wipe their tears, and lately, travel and discover other coasts. But in the realm of sex, the confusion between need and desire had become an erotic death sentence.

Later, Carl reported a few mini breakthroughs in which he connected with his manly desires. He felt in charge; he "knew" he wanted Joanna and their lovemaking felt full. One day, he came home with nail polish to give Joanna a pedicure. The color was dark, not a mommy color. Another day he brought a silk scarf to add texture to the softness and to blindfold her. One evening when she refused his advances, he took the scarf and used it to masturbate in front of her. The little boy who had a tantrum of despair and rejection now discovers that he can self-sooth in the presence of his wife. His imagination is flowing and play has replaced shame. Having found the pleasures of the "real," we were able to go back and examine Carl's historical quests for this exact encounter online.

Upon listening and probing the intricacies of the erotic imagination, therapists can uncover the shrewdness of fantasy, its energy, its artful efficiency, its healing qualities, and its psychological *tour de force.* Our fantasies combine the uniqueness of our personal history with the broad sweep of the collective cultural imagination: the incentives and the prohibitions, the ideals and the repressions, what we are told is sexy and what we are told is forbidden. They bridge the gap between the possible and the permissible.

Fantasy is the alchemy that turns this jumbled mishmash mixture of psychic ingredients into the pure gold of erotic arousal, a powerful antidote to libidinal demise in the relationship.

References

Bader, M. J. (2002). *Arousal: The secret logic of sexual fantasies*. New York, NY: St. Martin's.
Friday, N. (1992). *Men in love: Men's sexual fantasies: The triumph of love over rage*. New York, NY: Delta.
Morin, J. (1995). *The erotic mind.* New York, NY: Harper Collins.

Couples and Kinky Sexuality: The Need for a New Therapeutic Approach

Margaret Nichols

From the very start of psychiatric nomenclature, non-procreative sexual behaviors have tended to be viewed a priori as pathological: guilty until proven innocent. Today we look back on some of the diagnoses and harsh treatments used to "cure" people of what were considered deviant sexual behaviors and we shake our heads in wonder that our field could once have been so primitive. It is embarrassing to remember that our colleagues once endorsed cliterodectomies and forced sterilization, condemned masturbation and oral sex, and subjected people to electroshock therapy and lobotomies for sexual behaviors we now consider normal.

From a historical perspective, we should be deeply skeptical of psychiatric diagnoses involving sexuality, because the designations of "sick" and "healthy" seem to mirror rapidly changing social mores which calls into question the scientific basis for classification (Bayer 1981; Szasz 1961). Nymphomania, a diagnosis that applied only to women, was included in the first DSM in 1951 (APA 1951), during a time when our culture did not expect women to enjoy sex and deemed them defective if they did. As sexual standards for women (and everyone) became more liberal, so did diagnoses; the 1980s saw the DSM discard nymphomania but introduce HSDD (Hypoactive Sexual Desire Disorder) as the culture shifted from condemning women for being too sexual to pathologizing not being sexual enough (APA 1980).

Homosexuality is another prototypical example: before 1973, all manner of invasive and punitive treatment methods were acceptable to "cure" homosexuality; at this writing, most mental health professional organizations condemn reparative therapy as a cure for what is no longer considered an illness. Actually, some organizations even support gay marriage (Bayer 1981; Drescher and Zucker 2006). Recent decades have seen changes in the way gays, lesbians, bisexuals, and transgender people are viewed by mental health professionals, but this comparative enlightenment has not extended to the so-called "paraphilias." People whose sexual practices

Editors' note: First published in 2011, American Family Therapy Academy Monograph Series.

M. Nichols (✉)
Institute for Personal Growth, NJ, USA
e-mail: shrnklady@aol.com

T. Nelson, H. Winawer (eds.), *Critical Topics in Family Therapy*,
AFTA SpringerBriefs in Family Therapy, DOI 10.1007/978-3-319-03248-1_15,

are outside accepted norms have become increasingly visible in our culture and, to a lesser extent, in the offices of psychotherapists. The traditional psychiatric view of sexual minorities, however, has not changed. The mainstream view in the mental health field is still that non-standard sexual practices are pathologies that should be included in the diagnostic manual. This view is being challenged by a vocal minority of sexologists (Kleinplatz and Moser 2006; Moser 2001; Nichols 2006; Weinberg 2006).

Defining BDSM and Kinky Sex

BDSM is a modern acronym to denote certain sexual activities broadly described as bondage (B), dominance (D), submission (S), and sado-masochism (SM). Many would include fetishism as properly belonging to this group of sexual activities, and fetishists are considered part of the BDSM community. Collectively, these practices and attractions are sometimes referred to as "kinky." In general, kinky sexual activities include one or more of the following characteristics:

- A hierarchical power structure, that is, by mutual agreement, one person dominates and the other(s) submits. It is important to note that these roles are negotiated for sexual play in much the same way that kids agree on the roles of cops and robbers for the duration of the game.
- Intense stimulation usually associated with physical or emotional discomfort or pain, for example, slapping, humiliation.
- Forms of sexual stimulation involving mild sensory deprivation or sensory confusion (similar to that experienced on some amusement park rides) and/or the use of restraints, for example, bondage, use of blindfolds.
- Role-playing of fantasy sexual scenarios, for example, doctor-patient roles, abduction fantasies. The roles usually incorporate a dominant/subordinate theme, often mirroring roles commonly found in life such as teacher-student and boss-worker.
- Use of certain preferred objects and materials as sexual enhancers, for example, leather, latex, stiletto heels.
- Other unusual sexual objects or practices often classified as a fetish, for example, fixation with feet.

BDSM sexual activities share certain characteristics. First they are statistically non-normative, that is, they seem unusual to those who do not share BDSM proclivities. Second, during a sexual experience, called a scene, the roles appear very polarized (top/bottom, dominant/submissive). Third, BDSM players experiment with physical stimuli and emotions like fear, humiliation, or pain that have a paradoxical relationship to the pleasure of sex. BDSM activities are the extreme sports of sexuality. These sexual activities share much in common with activities like Iron Man competitions, a penchant for sky-diving, and a love of horror movies. The combination of pleasure with negative sensations is the hallmark of BDSM. It is the source of what is often called a "peak experience," which many believe is an essential quest of humans once basic needs have been met. Peak experiences can be experienced as spiritual, revelatory, and healing. A woman with a sexual abuse history who role plays a little girl with a partner who is sensitive and attentive to her history may enact a BDSM scene and may achieve intense sexual satisfaction, a sense of spiritual connection, and a healing of childhood wounds all at the same time. In fact, Kleinplatz (2006) has called BDSM practitioners "extraordinary lovers" who can teach the rest of us a great deal about romance, creativity, sexual bonding, and healing, as well as about keeping sex vibrant and authentic in long term relationships.

The "kink community" is a loose network of advocacy and support groups, spaces and events. The Internet has allowed people interested in BDSM to find each other and, over time, to create a network of real-world social organizations, to sponsor events and to organize political and advocacy groups. The social networking site Fetlife.com, similar to Facebook as a social networking site, began in 2008 and, as of this writing two years later, boasts half a million members. Leaders within the community have promulgated guidelines for what is considered acceptable BDSM practices. The motto of the community is "Safe, Sane, Consensual" (Wiseman 1996). Kinky activities quite specifically do not include, for example, rape or sexual contact with children. The intent is for all participants to be consenting adults who are fully informed and to avoid activities that might pose a medical or mental danger. Most community leaders frown upon the use of alcohol or recreational drugs by participants in BDSM activities.

Imposing unwanted danger, trauma or injury is as unrelated to BDSM as rape is to intercourse. Nevertheless, the [previous] Diagnostic and Statistical Manual, the DSM IV (APA 2000) classified Fetishism, Fetishistic Transvestitism, and Sadomasochism as mental illnesses with loose criteria for inclusion that people can be and are deemed mentally ill because their behavior upsets a spouse. And this has consequences. People who practice BDSM have lost jobs, housing, and custody of their children based on the testimony of psychiatric experts' pathologizing their sexual practices (Kleinplatz and Moser 2006; Wright 2006). BDSM clients report feeling abused at the hands of mental health professionals (Hoff and Sprott 2009). White (2006) reported that some people have been arrested for BDSM behaviors despite the dear consensual nature of their decision to participate in BDSM behaviors. Classifying behaviors as psychiatric diseases provided a psychological justification for oppressive discrimination. Thus, professional views of BDSM are deeply important not only to our clients but to society as a whole.

Both Moser and Kleinplatz (2006) and the National Coalition for Sexual Freedom (NCSF) White Paper on the DSM Revision (2010) provide comprehensive reviews of the scientific literature on BDSM. This literature clearly refutes most of the DSM-IV statements about paraphilias by exposing the lack of evidence for the APA's assertions. It is beyond the scope of this paper to expand on these arguments; interested readers are urged to read the above sources for a full perspective of the controversy. Revisions to the DSM-V[1] of the paraphilia section, which can be found at www.dsm5.org, reflect a major shift in the diagnosis, a shift that has been praised as well as condemned for not going far enough (Moser 2010). The DSM-5 clearly distinguishes between a paraphilic interest and a paraphilic disorder. It stipulates that BDSM activities are not pathological unless they cause distress or harm to self or others. Critics of this revision, like Moser and Kleinplatz (2005), point out the similarity between the "distress" criteria and the old category of ego-dystonic homosexuality that was removed from the DSM. Both ignore the likelihood that the "distress" of the paraphilia is socially caused, like the "distress" of homosexuality. According to these authors, the diagnoses still reflect socially negative attitudes toward an oppressed minority and reinforce that oppression.

What the Data Tell Us

The image of a person diagnosed with a paraphilic disorder as portrayed by the DSM-IV and most psychiatry texts is that of a socially isolated person at a low functioning job, with an impaired ability to sustain intimate relationships and a high likelihood of depression, anxiety, and personality disorder. This person is usually assumed to be male. His sexuality is supposedly narrowly focused on a particular fetish or behavior; he is compelled to engage in this behavior and he is driven to escalate his sexual activity to more intense levels. He ultimately progresses from consensual to nonconsensual acts (APA 2000). Paradoxically, according to the APA, although his sexual focus is narrow, he is also more likely to engage in multiple paraphilic behaviors including pedophilia. His impulse control is impaired and he is likely to engage in "frequent, unprotected sex … [that includes] infection with, or transmission of, a sexually transmitted disease… [and that incurs] injuries ranging in extent from minor to life threatening" (APA 2000, p. 567)

Shockingly, there is no scientific evidence beyond "clinical observation" to support this portrait (Moser 2001; Weinberg 2006). To the contrary, the few studies that actually include adults who engage in BDSM practices show results in direct contradiction to this stereotype. First, BDSM practices are not as rare as previously thought and are found among women at rates close to those for males. Janus and Janus (1993), in a national study of 2,800 respondents to a lengthy questionnaire asking about sexual practices, found that about 12 % of male and female respondents had engaged in some BDSM behavior. Moser and Kleinplatz (2006), reviewing multiple studies that attempted surveys of BDSM, estimated that about 10 % of adults have participated in these practices. Richters et al. (2008), in the only population-based prevalence study to date, found that about 2 % of respondents, male and female, had engaged in BDSM activities in the twelve months prior to the survey, greater than the percent who identified as gay. Both Cross and Matheson

[1] Editors' note: Since the first writing of this chapter, these revisions are in effect at the time of publication of this book (APA 2013).

(2006) and Weinberg (2006) concluded that SM practitioners have the same rates of mental illness and the same degree of psychological adjustment as nonpractitioners. And Richters and colleagues (2008), who included mental health measures in their survey, found identical rates of pathology in the BDSM sample compared to the non-BDSM respondents, but also reported a more diverse range of sexual activities in the BDSM practitioners. They concluded, "Our findings support the idea that BDSM is simply a sexual interest attractive to a minority, not a pathological symptom of past abuse or difficulty with 'normal' sex" (p. 1660).

Countertransference: If It is Not Sick, Why Does It Seem So Weird?

For many clinicians, negative countertransference is the greatest impediment to working with kinky clients. Despite the research findings, a few of us find it difficult to see BDSM as "normal" because some of the sexual behaviors seem strange, frightening, and inexplicable to many. Because of the difficulty in imagining how a particular activity can be genuinely pleasurable, the tendency is to judge its appeal as "sick." It is therefore helpful for therapists to try to gain a personal understanding of the appeal of BDSM. Many people can find something in their own personal experience that helps them understand BDSM practices. Those who have ever had sex someplace where it isn't "supposed" to take place—the in-laws' bathroom or the kitchen table—or fantasized having sex with someone "off limits" will understand the appeal of transgressive sex. People who have liked "dirty talk" during sex may understand how erotic a little bit of humiliation can be. Those who have experienced a hickey as erotic, enjoyed a love bite or love scratch, or liked having their hair pulled have a glimpse of dominance and submission, sensory distortion, and sado-masochism. Discovering that corsets, silk undergarments, or thongs are a turn-on is similar to the erotic pull of a fetish. Even if none of these experiences appeal to you, consider other activities where positive affect seems at first blush counterintuitive: horror movies, amusement park rides, extreme sports, car racing, zip gliding, boxing. These common experiences illustrate the fact that pleasure can come from many seemingly contradictory sources.

In working with people in the kink community, it is helpful to try to extend one's own experiences to find common ground. But sometimes this is difficult; there are times when a certain activity seems bizarre or repugnant, and it might be hard to not pathologize those who participate. People in the BDSM community have a word for this: it is called being *squicked. Squicked* is an invented word meant to connote an uncontrollable physical revulsion that includes no moral judgment. If you are strongly turned off to an activity and therefore decide that those who participate are "sick," you are exhibiting judgment. But if you are squicked, you may feel repulsed, but remain non-judgmental. When members of the BDSM community face this visceral reaction from others, they assume it might come from ignorance, a reaction formation to the other's own arousal, or simply an expression an idiosyncratic distaste. When a clinician is squicked, it is neither cause for alarm nor a reason to judge the client, but rather an opportunity to examine our own countertransference feelings, perhaps with a colleague or supervisor sensitive to BDSM issues. Clinicians who are troubled by their own reactions may also benefit from more information, such as one of the excellent books explaining and describing BDSM practices (Califia 2001; Morpheus 2008; Thompson 1992; Wiseman 1996).

Sometimes, understanding how a practice produces pleasurable sensations helps quell the squicked feeling. Steel nipple clamps can look frightening. But they make more sense when one understands that, once the clamps are removed, the nipple is left exquisitely sensitive. Spanking and flogging make sense as well in the context of the physiological phenomena induced by extremes of sensation. The flow of blood to the surface of the skin, the rush of endorphins and other chemicals, create an experience known to BDSM practitioners as "subspace" (i.e., a psychological submissive space), an experience often described as an out-of-body altered state like flying or floating weightless. This experience, which some people interpret as spiritual (Thompson 1992), can be deeply fulfilling on levels beyond sexual.

Another common barrier to understanding BDSM is the perceived need to explain the origin of the behavior. "Why would someone want to (fill in the blank: be a bottom, flog their partner, get tied up, etc.)?" The question itself is a subtle way of pathologizing behavior. Just as people want to know the origins of homosexuality but do not question how heterosexuality develops, we often assume a psychodynamic reason for nonstandard sexual practices. Therapists want to know why someone likes spankings, but not why they like oral sex. Therapists question why a man would want to urinate on a partner's body, but not why he wants to ejaculate on her. Before pursuing psychodynamic explanations for unusual sexual behavior, a therapist might ask herself whether she would do the same for more mundane sexuality.

How to Tell When a Behavior Really is Problematic

Therapists sometimes encounter cases where sexual behaviors really are problematic and/or pathological. Some of these situations are easy to discern, like rape or child sexual abuse. Other behaviors, however, require contextual assessment: when does someone have a sex addiction and when are they merely very sexual beings? Sexual issues, like other socially charged concerns (How much drinking is too much? When is child corporal punishment a form of abuse?), evades simple agreement, even among experts. This problem may arise more often for clinicians relatively less experienced in working with BDSM practitioners. The clinician may not automatically know if a behavior is safe or sane, two of the three criteria for appropriate BDSM activity. Many of us harbor unconscious biases regarding sexual risks as compared to other, more common risks. We often tend to accept common risks more than uncommon ones, for example, the risk of allowing a child to play football.

Most clinicians, at least those who have training in domestic violence, will have more ability to assess the third component, consensuality. One of its key aspects is mutual enjoyment. The difference between a violent sexual sadist and a sadist in the BDSM community is that the former has no interest in the needs or well-being of their partner, while sadists in the BDSM world usually pride themselves on how well they take care of their "bottoms." Mutually arousing and agreed-upon sexual activities are consensual. Nonconsensual BDSM relationships are a particular form of partner/spousal abuse, and this abuse is marked by the lack of pleasure and the presence of real fear on the part of the submissive partner, a fear that is not confined to the sexual encounter, but pervades the relationship. When consensuality is not obvious, the therapist can assess the couple for domestic violence. It is also important to recognize that domestic abuse can occur toward the more dominant partner from the one who is more submissive. The therapist should interview the partners separately to assess safety and look for nonsexual violence as well as evidence of rage and/or contempt for the partner. The therapist can assess for signs of fear and intimidation, incidence of nonsexual abuse, and a sense of being trapped in the relationship.

Resources and Suggestions for Working With BDSM Clients

As therapists begin to work with clients practicing BDSM, they may be comfortable having an affirmative stance but not yet ready for complex cases. There are numerous resources available for therapists wanting to develop a more kink-friendly practice. Communities often have local resources that may not be well known, including colleagues with experience working with the BDSM community who are available for supervision. A national listing of providers is available through KAP (Kink Aware Professionals), a referral directory listed on the NCSFreedom.org website. Additionally, clinicians who desire more training in how to better serve BDSM clients can contact CARAS (Community Academic Consortium for Research on Alternative Sexualities) and can view their DVD on dialed "do's and don'ts" as a way to begin. CARAS also provides special programs given through sex therapy organizations like the American Association of Sex Educators, Counselors, and Therapists (AASECT: www.aasect.org).

The belief that BDSM behavior automatically needs to be assessed for clinical significance is itself a biased belief. Ironically, a therapist might best display sensitivity by not bringing BDSM into the therapy when it is not warranted. In general, it is unwarranted unless the client brings it up as a problem. Hoff and Sprott (2009), in a study of the therapy experiences of members of the BDSM community, found that many people were critical of therapists who they perceived to be voyeur because they kept inquiring about sex when it was not part of the presenting problem. Positive BDSM experiences can, however, be highlighted for couples where they exemplify connection and collaborative communication.

Occasionally BDSM practitioners come into therapy needing assistance with advocacy. BDSM activities are still pathologized and misunderstood, and in some parts of the country BDSM sexual play is viewed as spousal abuse. The partner of a spouse with visible minimal bruises may be automatically arrested and charged with assault, even if both partners maintain that the sexual activity that produced these bruises was consensual. There are occasions when child welfare organizations remove children from the home of the parents because of BDSM activities, or when such activities are used in divorce suits to challenge custody or visitation. A therapist can play an important role in these situations by being willing to give affidavits or court testimony in support of the couple and in defense of their sexual preferences.

Individual therapists may also encounter clients who have internalized societal stigmatization of BDSM, who express self-hatred, and may even ask to be cured. Hearing a therapist officially state that their sexual behavior is not an illness can be an incredibly powerful experience. Encouraging such clients to view their self-hatred as socially induced may liberate them to accept their own sexual behaviors. Finally, some therapists refuse to help clients rid themselves of their paraphilia, believing that, like homosexuality, it is nearly impossible to extinguish strong, specific sexual desires.

By far the most common problem a couple and family therapist will encounter when working with BDSM clients is marital discord following the revelation that one partner is kinky. Just as, for example, some gay men still repudiate their own sexuality and mask their orientation behind a heterosexual family, many people with kinky orientations do the same. These clients hide their sexual preferences from their spouses and may or may not practice them in secret. Sometimes they are "found out," and sometimes they themselves come to abhor the deception inherent in their double lives and desire a fuller and more honest expression of their sexuality. The traditional treatment for these couples has been to label the BDSM partner's behavior as pathological, both as a paraphilia and as infidelity. Attempts are made to cure the transgressing partner of his or her desires, or at least to convince him or her to suppress them. Sometimes the BDSM partner enthusiastically endorses this approach, internalizing the view that the behavior is "sick."

A different approach is, first, to separate out the issues of fidelity and of sexual preference, and, second, to normalize the sexual behavior of the BDSM partner and frame the situation as a (possible) mismatch of sexual scripts. Of course, if the BDSM partner has engaged in secret activities, many of the issues of betrayal and mistrust are the same as those encountered when one partner has had an affair. But there is an important difference. The BDSM partner may be more like a gay man who has spent a lifetime avoiding his sexual orientation than he is like a cheating spouse. Even if the partner forgives the infidelity, it will not be very effective to simply dismiss the BDSM sexual preferences. The partner who feels betrayed has far more to deal with than the partner of someone who has had an affair. He or she must not only cope with the pain and shock of infidelity, but also confront the reality that, as partners, they have sexual differences that may not be resolvable. The partner of the BDSM-oriented individual has been deceived on a much deeper level; one partner has concealed fundamental parts of his or her identity, not just sexual behavior, even if the deception has been wholly a by-product of the lack of readiness to cope with ego-dystonic sexual desires. The couple faces a number of threats to their integrity, and the therapist must shepherd the relationship through what will certainly be a profound transformation. However, it is not usually necessary to deconstruct the relationship to understand what "caused" the sexual straying. Many couples in this situation have admirably intact relationships in other respects, and the revelation of the BDSM partners secret life probably has more to do with chance than with relationship dynamics. Working with these couples can be deeply rewarding because couples can become more creative in finding common sexual interests. If the romantic or sexual component cannot be salvaged, some marriages can successfully transform into close and affectionate friendships.

Clinical Vignette

Michael, a man in his mid-thirties who had been married for ten years to a woman he adored, consulted me in great distress about what he initially presented as a problem with erectile dysfunction. Within the first session it became clear that his erectile difficulties were related to his suppression of his intense desires to be placed in bondage. While he enjoyed more common forms of sex (which he called "vanilla sex," as many members of the BDSM community do), his secret, unfulfilled wish to be a "bondage bottom" gradually dominated his thoughts, disrupting his ability to function sexually with his wife. Michael had never revealed his interests to Judy because he was sure they would repel her.

When Judy was brought into therapy sessions, she initially reacted with confusion, shock, and a sense of being betrayed. The psychoeducation I provided helped her accept the idea that Michael was not "sick." While metaphorically comparing Michael's situation to one of a closeted gay man helped her feel less personally betrayed, she still felt some repugnance for the sexual behaviors he desired. However, the two partners had an extremely strong bond, a great deal of quality intimacy, and both were strongly motivated to work through this problem.

Through individual sessions that included the use of EMDR to help Judy resolve her own childhood abuse issues, Judy lost the sense of distaste she had about Michael's sexual interests. She became curious and open to experimentation, and together the partners enacted some of Michael's fantasies. To her surprise, Judy found that she was not only able to tolerate being a "bondage top," putting Michael in restraints and controlling his behavior in a sexual situation, she discovered that this role produced a powerful sexual high for her as well. Several years later, they still periodically update me. The two continue to enjoy this sexual behavior and have connected with others in the kink community by participating in BDSM events.

Not all such situations have such happy resolutions. Some couples with discordant sexual preferences do not find a satisfying agreement and choose to part. But even when the outcome of therapy is divorce or separation, much can be accomplished. The therapist can help the BDSM partner rid him- or herself of shame and can keep the non-kinky partner from personalizing and blaming him- or herself for the partner's sexuality. Child custody and visitation issues can be prevented from becoming enmeshed with the partner's sexual behavior. In some future world, we may all understand and accept our diverse sexualities at an earlier age, before we enter serious, committed relationships. But in this world, a couple and family therapist can help prevent an unfortunate situation created by stigmatization of non-normative sexuality from becoming a tragedy that destroys both partners in a relationship.

References

American Psychiatric Association. (1951). *Diagnostic and statistical manual of mental disorders.* Washington, DC: American Psychiatric Association.

American Psychiatric Association. (1980). *Diagnostic and statistical manual of mental disorders* (3rd ed.). Washington, DC: American Psychiatric Association.

American Psychiatric Association. (2000). *Diagnostic and statistical manual of mental disorders (*4th ed.). Washington, DC: American Psychiatric Association.

American Psychiatric Association. (2013). *Diagnostic and statistical manual of mental disorders* (5th ed.). Washington, DC: American Psychiatric Association.

Bayer, R. (1981). *Homosexuality and American* psychiatry. New York, NY: Basic Books.

Califia, P. (2001). *Sensuous magic: A guide to SIM for adventurous couples*. San Francisco, CA: Cleis Press.

Cross, P., & Matheson, K. (2006). Understanding sadomasochism: An empirical examination *of* four perspectives. *Journal of Homosexuality*, 50(2/3), 133–166.

Drescher, J., & Zucker, K. (2006). *Ex-gay research: Analyzing the Spitzer study and its relation to politics, religion, science, and culture*. New York, NY: Harrington.

Hoff, G., & Sprott, R. (2009).Therapy experiences of clients with BDSM sexualities: Listening to a stigmatized sexuality. *Electronic Journal of Human Sexuality, 12*. www.ejhs.org/Volume12/bdsm.htm. Accessed 30 Sept. 2009.

Janus, S. S., & Janus, C. L. (1993). *The Janus Report*. New York, NY: Wiley and Sons.

Kleinplatz, P. J. (2006). Learning from extraordinary lovers: Lessons from the edge. *Journal of Homosexuality, 50*(2–3), 325–345.

Kleinplatz, M., & Moser, C. (2006). SM (sadomasochistic) interests as an issue in a child custody proceeding. *Journal of Homosexuality, 50*(2/3), 233–243.

Morpheus. (2008). How *to be kinky: A beginner's guide to BDSM*. San Francisco, CA: Green Candy Press.

Moser, C. (2001). Paraphilia: A critique of a confused concept. In *New directions in sex therapy innovations and alternatives*, ed. P. Kleinplatz, 91–108. Philadelphia, PA: Brunner-Routledge.

Moser, C. (2010). Problems with ascertainment. *Archives of Sexual Behavior, 39*, 1225–1227.

Moser, C., & Kleinplatz, P. (2005). DSM-IV-TR and the paraphilias: An argument for removal. *Journal of Psychology & Human Sexuality, 17*(3/4), 91–109.

Moser, C., & Kleinplatz, P. (2006). Introduction: The state of our knowledge on S/M. *Journal of Homosexuality, 50*(2/3), 1–15.

NCSF. (2010). White paper on the DSM revision. www.ncsfreedom.org. Accessed Aug 2010.

Nichols, M. (2006). Psychotherapeutic issues with "kinky" clients: Clinical problems, yours and theirs. *Journal of Homosexuality, 50*(2/3), 281–300.

Richters, J., de Visser, R., Rissel, C., Grulich, A., & Smith, A. (2008). Demographic and psychosocial features of participants in bondage and discipline, "sadomasochism" or dominance and submission (BDSM): Data from a national survey. *Journal of Sexual Medicine*, *5*(7), 1660–1668.

Szasz, T. (1961). *The myth of mental illness*. New York, NY: Harper.

Thompson, M. (1992). Leatherfolk: *Radical sex, people, politics, and practice*. Boston, MA: Alyson Books.

Weinberg, T. S. (2006). Sadomasochism and the social sciences: A review of the sociological and social psychological literature. *Journal of Homosexuality*, *50*(2/3), 17–40.

White, C. (2006). The Spanner trials and the changing law on sadomasochism in the UK. *Journal of Homosexuality*, *50*(2/3), 167–188.

Wiseman, J. (1996). *SM101: A realistic introduction*. San Francisco, CA: Greenery Press.

Wright, S. (2006). Discrimination of SM-identified individuals. *Journal of Homosexuality*, *50*(2/3), 217–231.

Open Relationships: A Culturally and Clinically Sensitive Approach

Deanna M. Fierman and Shruti Singh Poulsen

Consensual romantic and sexual relationships that are open and nonmonogamous challenge the norms of exclusive relationships and have largely been overlooked by the scholarly literature (Ellis 1970; LaSala 2004; Otto 1970; Rubin 2001; Weitzman 2007) including the couple and family therapy literature. An integration of current theories of couple and family counseling must be adapted to include open relationships because these relationships are becoming more prevalent and visible (Taormino 2008; Nelson 2010; Weitzman 2007). People in open relationships may be discouraged at the difficulty of finding culturally sensitive therapists (Keener 2004; Shernoff 2006) and are concerned both about being judged by the therapist and with the need to educate the therapist about open relationships.

There has been scant research on both the prevalence of open relationships and on the ways monogamous values affect therapists' work with consensually nonmonogamous clients. This is complicated by the difficulty of conducting research on sexual minority populations (Shernoff 2006). Informal surveys about nonmonogamy suggest it may be more common than most people assume (Cook 2004). For example, the Janus Report (Janus and Janus 1993), a survey of human sexual and erotic behavior, analyzed 2,765 questionnaires and follow-up interviews nationwide and found that 21 % of adult respondents reported participating in an open marriage (Taormino 2008). Another study examining bisexually-identified men and women showed that out of 217 bisexual people, 33 % reported that they were in open relationships, and 54 % considered polyamory an ideal relationship model (Taormino 2008). In addition, an on-line survey of over 14,000 people conducted by Oprah.com revealed that 14 % of men and 7 % of women surveyed were in an open marriage (The Oprah Winfrey Show 2006). Although these surveys lack rigorous

Editors' note: First published in 2011, American Family Therapy Academy Monograph Series.

D. M. Fierman (✉)
University of Colorado Boulder, Boulder, CO, USA
e-mail: deanna.fierman@gmail.com

S. S. Poulsen
University of Colorado Denver, Denver, CO, USA

T. Nelson, H. Winawer (eds.), *Critical Topics in Family Therapy*,
AFTA SpringerBriefs in Family Therapy, DOI 10.1007/978-3-319-03248-1_16,

scientific methodology, they reveal an increasing interest in, or at least visibility of, open relationships.

Open relationship structures may take many forms. These include, but are not limited to, *partnered nonmonogamy*, *swinging*, *polyamory*, and *monogamous/nonmonogamous combinations* (Easton and Liszt 1997; Shernoff 2006; Taormino 2008). These relationship structures are all consensual, which is a distinction integral to understanding how alternative relationships differ from infidelity or cheating (LaSala 2004). Cheating can certainly occur in open relationships as it can in any relationship; for example, a partner may maintain a secret relationship or give misleading information about the nature of that relationship despite agreeing to disclose all romantic or sexual interactions.

People in open relationships sometimes identify one partner as their *primary partner*. *Partnered nonmonogamy* generally emphasizes a nonmonogamous sexual relationship while the emotional intimacy remains with the primary partner. *Swinging*, in contrast, is considered more of a lifestyle with distinct social etiquette and formal events rather than a purely sexual practice, though it is similar to partnered nonmonogamy in that participants are generally emotionally monogamous and sexually nonmonogamous. *Polyamory* refers to having multiple emotionally intimate relationships simultaneously. Often, though not always, these relationships are sexual in nature; the emphasis in polyamory is generally on the presence of multiple romantic partners. *Polyfidelity* refers to a group of three or more people in a closed relationship. As Taormino (2008) points out, the aforementioned categories contain false dichotomies; clients can belong to several of the categories. For example, a polyamorous couple may also choose to participate in the swinging community (Cook 2004), or an initially polyfidelitous triad might later choose to have an emotionally closed but sexually open relationship. However, these labels are useful for the purposes of discussion.

Culturally and Contextually Sensitive Practice

Contextually and culturally sensitive practices can be implemented in practical yet meaningful ways. Intake forms and assessments can be changed to reflect diversity of relationships; for example, rather than ask clients to specify "Marital Status," the more inclusive "Relationship Status" could be used, including options other than two-person relationship formats. Similarly, it may be possible to raise awareness of open relationships by using inclusive language in the therapy literature.

A number of concepts exist in the literature on open relationships that are useful for therapists. Although the concepts of *compersion* and *starvation economies*, the myths of equality, institutional and social prejudices, and jealousy are certainly not unique to clients in open relationships, they may be especially likely to arise when working with these clients. Therefore, a discussion of these concepts may be particularly useful for therapists working with this population.

Compersion

Those who are in open relationships often have nontraditional feelings toward their partners' other romantic or sexual relationships. One of these is *compersion*, a term coined by the Kerista commune in San Francisco, which occurs when one partner has positive feelings about a partner's other intimate relationships (Cook 2004; Taormino 2008). Compersion can be similar to being happy because one's partner develops a new friendship, a hobby, or other outside interest. Although the idea of finding joy by observing your partner's joy may be a familiar concept, helping a client find joy in her partner's other relationships is something clinicians may overlook. Therapists need to spend time exploring and engaging their own relationship with the concept of compersion in order to successfully work with clients in open relationships, and this process will look different for each individual. It is essential that therapists who work with these clients develop an under-standing of compersion as a mentally and emotionally sound way to respond to one's partner. Naturally, compersion isn't always possible or desirable. However, it could be a useful part of reframing the partners' bond and strengthening the connection of a primary relationship (Cook 2004).

Starvation Economy

Another somewhat distinctive concern to those in alternative relationships is that of the *starvation economy* (Easton and Liszt 1997), or the worry that there is only a limited amount of a substance. This is indeed the case for many things, including time with a partner and their sexual or emotional energy.

In addition, many intimate relationships are rooted in the idea that there can only be so much love available, thereby conceptualizing love as a starvation economy. However, love for one person doesn't mean there must be any less love for another. Easton and Listz (1997) cite the example of a parent having plenty of love for multiple children, even when sufficient time or energy may be lacking. Thus, when counseling clients in an open relationship, it is important to identify and address the nature of a client's fear. Deconstructing this fear, placing it into a framework that helps the partners identify their specific concerns and see different perspectives, renders the fear more manageable.

For example, a client may be unhappy because her husband spends a great deal of time with another partner. The therapist might inquire whether she feels as though she is losing her husband's affection, his time, or both. Depending on the client's response, the therapist might encourage her to discuss her concerns of loss of affection, mediate a conversation about time management, explore their narratives about the relationship between time and love, and inquire how experiences have shaped the clients' ability to handle multiple demands on their attention.

Myth of Equality

Many clients in open relationships unwittingly fall into believing the *myth of equality* (Taormino 2008), which assumes that each partner has the same needs and desires. Taormino discusses how the concept of equality has become a central part of relationships, and explains that equality has become synonymous with symmetry in modern parlance. In reality, partners in an open relationship are likely to have different needs in terms of style of open relationship, amount of information they want to be told, sexual behavior, and so forth. Partners may incorrectly assume that their needs are the same and conclude that they necessarily must share the same set of behavioral rules. Unnecessary conflict could arise when, for example, partners differ in the degree to which they want to hear about the other's sexual encounters.

In the above example, it may make sense for one party to give information about sexual behavior or emotional intimacy and for the other to refrain from giving any. There is nothing wrong with asymmetric information sharing as long as both partners agree to the arrangement. Clients will thus be working within the reality of their own particular relationship, rather than within a prescribed framework.

Jealousy

Jealousy is a complex force in relationships, consisting of conflicting emotions, thoughts, and actions (Sheinkman and Werneck 2010). Jealousy is experienced in both monogamous and open relationships. It is important to note, however, that those who choose open relationships are not predisposed to feel jealousy any more or less than those who choose monogamy (Easton and Liszt 1997). Within the literature on alternative relationships, jealousy is not perceived as inherently negative or positive; rather, it is viewed as an emotion that needs to be acknowledged and worked through in the context of a relationship (Easton and Liszt 1997; Taormino 2008). People in open relationships often acknowledge early on that jealousy is likely to arise and choose to actively explore this concern, rather than deciding to end a relationship because of the presence of jealousy (Cook 2004).

Therapists may be of great assistance in exploring the issue of jealousy as long as they understand that the goal is *not* to encourage clients to be monogamous. Rather, the goal might be to help communicate and manage jealousy effectively. Facing the emotions surrounding jealousy is just as crucial for healing as addressing the behavior that provoked the jealousy, especially if the behavior had been mutually agreed upon and if the partners wish to remain open. Therapists should be cautioned not to assume that a behavior causing jealousy should necessarily be stopped.

Institutional and Social Prejudice

Like many minorities, people in open relationships face a number of visible and invisible external challenges (Shernoff 2006). We, as therapists, must not dismiss the ways that monogamy forms the implicit normative assumptions for all relationships in western cultures. Legal and medical authorities in the US assume families form a dyadic relationship structure. For example, three individuals in a committed triadic relationship are unable to establish legal parental rights for each adult. Social discrimination is widespread as well: it is found in the media, which almost exclusively depicts couples in closed relationships, and in everyday social assumptions, such as in the expectation that a person will have a single date at a social gathering. Keener (2004) explains that open relationships can be socially isolating due to their invisibility, and identifies six common fears: loss of friendships, potential for others' "freaking out," prejudice against and confusion with polygamy, the use of polyamory as a scapegoat, a lack of understanding, and the fear that others simply do not want to hear about nonmonogamous behavior.

The therapeutic environment is not immune from these underlying social assumptions (Shernoff 2006). Therapy will only be effective when ideas of normality and pathology are critically explored and deconstructed and when the therapist has examined her own biases (Nichols and Shernoff 2007). A constructionist viewpoint considers relational norms in the context of the social group in which they exist, enables acceptance of a client's story at face value, and also allows for challenging and restructuring realities and narratives that have the potential to harm the client or others (Nichols and Schwartz 2008; Pare 1995). For someone unfamiliar with the nonmonogamous community, many of the aforementioned challenges clients face due to institutional and social prejudice may, at first, be difficult to see. In addition to becoming educated about the social and legal concerns that people in open relationships encounter, therapists may choose to make explicitly clear to clients that they are familiar with open relationships and are comfortable exploring the topic during therapy.

Ethical Considerations

A number of ethical issues may arise for therapists who are approached by nonmonogamous clients. In some ways nonmonogamy is not particularly different from any other multicultural issue. However, the perspective that it is appropriate to have multiple sexual and romantic partners may be an especially difficult for some therapists, given how prevalent monogamy is in our society. One primary concern is how to approach therapy when clients' sexual or romantic proclivities do not align with the therapist's values. The legal and ethical implications of working with gay and lesbian clients when a therapist is not comfortable with homosexuality has been discussed in the therapeutic literature (Hermann and Herlihy 2006), and the concerns related to therapy with nonmonogamous clients are similar. It may be difficult for a therapist to discern how to broach the topic with clients or whether and when it is ethical to refer clients to another therapist due to discomfort or lack of experience with this population. Simply being aware of the possibility of seeing clients who are in open relationships and having referrals available to therapists who are comfortable with nonmonogamy can be an extremely important measure of support. Doing so demonstrates respect for a population that might otherwise easily be scared away from therapy due to past exposure to institutional prejudice (Keener 2004).

If a therapist is comfortable working with nonmonogamous clients, it may be helpful to give forethought as to how to broach the topic during therapy. There are small ways a therapist can explicitly demonstrate respect for this population, such as reformatting wording and questions on intake forms to be inclusive of open relationships, or adding a question that asks about the topic directly. It may also be useful to have a book on open relationships visible to provide clients with a way to bring up the topic of nonmonogamy. A therapist may also address the topic of open relationships while addressing general multicultural differences at the beginning of therapy, either directly or indirectly. A respectful statement about differences in worldview during a first session could help clients disclose their open relationships. For example, a therapist could encourage a client by saying, "I believe it is important to discuss how the lenses through which we see the world may differ. Our different experiences impact the way we view the world, and factors such as our gender, race, sexual orientation, and so forth can shape our perspective. I hope to honor your worldview in our work together. If I do or say something that feels as though it doesn't fit for you, I invite you to let me know so that we can address it."

Clinical Application

Exploring Nonmonogamy

When they came to therapy, Kay and Jim, both in their late twenties, reported they had been living together in a monogamous relationship for two years. They each identified as "primarily heterosexual" in their orientation and identified as White for their ethnic identity. Kay and Jim were in the process of exploring the option of an open relationship. Kay and Jim presented a recent incident in which they had mutually agreed to include a third individual in their sexual activities while still considering their own relationship as primary. Other than the occasional mutual fantasizing of including another individual in their sexual activity, neither had engaged in an intimate relationship with someone outside their relationship. Kay and Jim attributed their frequent arguments, lessening of positive interactions, and increasing tensions to the fact that they had not adequately addressed their goals and desires for a nonmonogamous relationship and had moved too quickly into an open sexual relationship. Their agreed on purpose for attending therapy was to understand what had happened to their relationship and to stabilize their relationship so that they might work toward their original goal of having a sexually and emotionally open relationship. Kay and Jim's tension had rapidly deteriorated into much anger, hurt and vilification of each other. They were concerned that just as they started considering an open relationship, difficulties began to emerge. They feared they would never be able to successfully engage in open relationships in the future, and that they might be unable to stay together.

Over the next few weeks, the therapist worked to make sessions productive for Kay and Jim by interrupting their personal attacks, offering process comments (e.g., in-the-moment comments that highlighted their verbal and nonverbal communication patterns, noting their patterns of interacting and pointing out when they were able to risk new behaviors, etc.), setting ground rules, and coaching them on speaking and listening skills. The therapist continued to explore the messages that the partners had received from their respective families of origin and from their cultural contexts. These messages were that monogamy was the only right way to engage in an intimate relationship, that having additional partners in a relationship constituted infidelity, and that relationships that veered from the norm were destined to fail. While exploring these messages, each partner was able to recognize that they had no relationship role models for what they desired in their own relationship. They also had few resources in their familial and social contexts for support, approval, or validation. As the partners' awareness of these challenges expanded, they were able to consider other ways of viewing the difficulties in their relationship. For example, they acknowledged that their relationship had been experiencing more stress because they were not automatically (as they might in other situations) turning to even a close friend or family member for advice or support due to the fear that they would be misunderstood, rejected, or vilified for their decision to have an open relationship. Gaining this additional awareness and understanding helped each develop a little more empathy and kindness for themselves and each other.

No one specific model of therapy was used to work with this couple; the therapist used practices of therapy that would be considered structural (Dickerson 2010) but were applied in a manner that reflected post-modern and constructionist elements and that attended to the clients' meaning and experiences. For example, the use of the genogram helped explore their family backgrounds, patterns, and messages, cultural narratives and experiences, and also their sexual, relational, and emotional experiences. In the process of constructing the genogram, the therapist asked each partner to identify their family-of- origin and cultural messages about the value of monogamy as a prerequisite for a successful intimate relationship, and about the meaning of love and commitment. In acknowledging the pressure of messages that challenged the credibility of open relationships, and exploring them in more depth, the couple reported feeling less "wrong" in their decision to move toward an open relationship because they were able to see that they held very different values and beliefs than their families of origin and their cultural contexts.

Seeing these differences starkly portrayed in the visual of their genogram also helped them recognize that their desire for an open relationship had no precedence or support in their families of origin. Thus, as a couple, they were trying to accomplish something in their relationship for which they had no role models. With this realization, each partner could take a stance that was less reactive and blaming toward the other. In creating the genogram, the therapist took a narrative and constructionist approach to create a therapeutic environment that felt safer and allowed each partner's experiences, meanings, and voices to be heard. While Kay and Jim sought therapy after a critical event and were highly escalated initially, the narratives that emerged through the genogram helped them de-escalate and be more open to each other's emotional experience and needs.

The therapist also fostered the couple's sense of safety and trust in their primary relationship by exploring the principles of the starvation economy, the myth of equality, the management of jealousy, and the ways in which these experiences could become sources of strength. Constructionist (Pare 1995) and narrative processes (Freedman and Combs 1996) such as contextualizing the clients' reactions to the precipitating event within the framework of their relationship experiences and their familial and cultural backgrounds helped the partners access their emotions, clearly express their emotional experiences and their needs, and develop a sense of empathy and understanding for each other even while dealing with the fact that their fear did not completely abate over the course of therapy (Johnson 2004).

While each partner wanted to move forward with the prospect of engaging in an open relationship, exploring their individual and conjoint narratives was a key part of the therapeutic process. Exploration of their family and cultural narratives enabled the couple to examine their conflict in a way that reduced blame toward each other. Their efforts shifted toward working together to create a new kind of relationship they both desired. A culturally and contextually sensitive approach using the genogram (McGoldrick et al. 2008), narrative therapy (Freedman and Combs 1996), and some Emotionally Focused Therapy (Johnson 2004) processes provided an initial opportunity to develop a new narrative that included understanding both the couple's initial reactivity and their reasons for wanting an open relationship. This, in turn, facilitated the development of new solutions and problem-solving skills.

Negotiating Nonmonogamy

In addition to the exploration of clients' cultural and familial expectations, their histories, and what an open relationship means to them, it is also important to examine the practicalities of an open relationship. By exploring their families of origin, the couple saw that they had neither support nor role models for the different kind of relationship they were trying to establish. This scenario is likely the case for many clients attempting an open relationship. Therapists have several options in working with clients to find resources and develop support systems. Therapists can suggest that clients actively seek out others in open relationships for support and friendship and can promote the use of online resources in finding information and communities. Clients may be encouraged to seek out self-growth opportunities that support the option of open relationships. In addition, therapists can act as role models for the clients by encouraging communication and introducing questions that help the partners define their relationship.

Although clients must discuss and set their own boundaries within their relationships, therapists can guide this conversation by asking culturally sensitive questions that include both behavioral and emotional components (Shernoff 2006). Behavioral components could include a discussion of when flirtation with others is appropriate, when and how frequently date nights could happen, with whom it is acceptable to have sexual encounters, which sexual behaviors are permissible, what type of fluid barriers will be used, sleeping arrangements, and so forth.

Kay and Jim discussed these concerns in their attempt to create a sense of trust and safety for each other in the relationship. The topic of a starvation economy may be particularly relevant when exploring behavior with clients because discussion about what behaviors are and are not acceptable may relate to a perception that a given substance is limited. During therapy, Kay and Jim realized they had been taught that sexual attraction is finite and that their jealousy was partially rooted in the fear of loss of the other's sexual desire.

Exploring clients' emotions in conjunction with their behaviors is clearly important. The topics of jealousy, insecurity, attachment, and compersion may arise when clients are discussing their open relationship. During the construction of the genogram, the messages that Kay and Jim learned from their families of origin began to emerge. Placing these messages and emotions in the context of a present-day situation can draw attention to specific issues that are likely to arise. For example, a therapist could ask a client to imagine his emotions when his primary partner is out on a date, and could explore these feelings with the clients while both are present. The therapist might inquire how the client expects he would feel as his primary partner is leaving on the date, may choose to explore whether a client desires reassurance during the time that a partner is on the date, and could discuss how the couple might choose to reconnect after a partner arrives home. Clients may also struggle with strong emotions relating to discrimination or a feeling of invisibility because of their open relationship.

In addition, it could be useful for a therapist to mediate a discussion on how to have a conversation with one's primary partner about the development of another intimate relationship and to explore what details will be shared. Clearly, it is impossible to plan for every eventuality, but general guidelines can certainly be developed. Reminding clients that misunderstandings will happen, and encouraging them to view misunderstandings as opportunities to clarify expectations will help to strengthen their relationship in whatever form it takes (Cook 2004).

Conclusion

To create a successful and fulfilling therapeutic experience for clients in open relationships, it is important to foster a safe and secure therapeutic environment that is rooted in the clients' reality. Therapists may join more easily with clients and become more effective in their clinical roles by becoming knowledgeable about constructs intrinsic to open relationships, by assessing how prepared they feel to work with clients from this population, and by examining their own comfort with the topic. Therapists should strive to create a space where clients' worldviews are readily accepted and where disclosure of open relationships is encouraged; this practice will allow the therapist to assess for referral needs early in the therapeutic relationship. When working with nonmonogamous clients, therapists should encourage explicit discussions of open relationships and the concepts of compersion, starvation economies, the myth of equality, institutional and social prejudices, and jealousy. Future work in this area should explore in greater detail which therapeutic approaches work most effectively with clients in open relationships, and whether the effectiveness of the therapeutic approach depends upon the structure of the open relationship.

References

Cook, E. (2004). Commitment in polyamory. *Electronic Journal of Human Sexuality*. http://www.ejhs.org/ volume8/cook1.html

Dickerson, V. (2010). Positioning oneself within an epistemology: Refining our thinking about integrative approaches. *Family Process*, *49*(3), 349–368. doi:10.1111/j.1545-5300.2010.01327.x

Easton, D., & Liszt, C. (1997). *The ethical slut*. San Francisco, CA: Greenery Press.

Ellis, A. (1970). Group marriage: A possible alternative? In H. A. Otto (Ed.), *The family in search of a future* (pp. 85–87). Norwalk, CT: Appleton-Century-Crofts.

Freedman, J. & Combs, G. (1996). *Narrative therapy: The social construction of preferred realities*. New York, NY: W.W. Norton.

Hermann, M. A., & Herlihy, B. R. (2006). Legal and ethical implications of refusing to counsel homosexual clients. *Journal of Counseling and Development*, *84*(4), 414–418.

Janus, S. S., & Janus, C. L. (1993). *The Janus Report on sexual behavior*. New York, NY: John Wiley.

Johnson, S. M. (2004). *The practice of emotionally focused couple therapy: Creating connection* (2nd ed.). New York, NY: Taylor & Francis.

Keener, M. C. (2004). *A phenomenology of polyamorous persons*. (Unpublished master's thesis). Salt Lake City, UT: University of Utah.

LaSala, M. C. (2004). Extradyadic sex and gay male couples: Comparing monogamous and nonmonogamous relationships. *Families in Society: The Journal of Contemporary Human Services*, *85*, 405–412.

McGoldrick, M., Gerson, R., & Petry, S. (2008). *Genograms: Assessment and intervention* (3rd ed.). New York, NY: W. W. Norton.

Nelson, T. (2010). The new monogamy. *Psychotherapy Networker, July/August 2010*. http://www.psychotherapynetworker.org/magazine/currentissue/926-the-new-monogamy

Nichols, M. P., & Schwartz, R. C. (2008). *Family therapy: Concepts and methods* (8th ed.). New York, NY: Allyn and Bacon.

Nichols, M., & Shernoff, M. (2007). Therapy with sexual minorities: Queering practice. In S. R. Leiblum (Ed.), *Principles and practice of sex therapy* (pp. 379–416). New York, NY: Guilford. doi:616.85'8306-dc.22

Otto, H. A. (1970). *The family in search of a future*. Norwalk, CT: Appleton-Century-Crofts.

Pare, D. (1995). Of families and other cultures: The shifting paradigm of family therapy. *Family Process*, *34*(1), 1–20.

Rubin, R. H. (2001). Alternative lifestyles revisited, or whatever happened to swingers, group marriages, and communes? *Journal of Family Issues*, *22*(6), 711–726. doi:10:1177/019251301022006003

Scheinkman, M., & Werneck, D. (2010). Disarming jealousy in couples relationships: A multidimensional approach. *Family Process*, *49*(4), 486–502. doi: 10.1111/j.1545-5300.2010.01335.x

Shernoff, M. (2006). Negotiated nonmonogamy and male couples. *Family Process*, *45*(4), 407–418.

Taormino, T. (2008). *Opening up: A guide to creating and sustaining open relationships*. San Francisco: Cleis Press. doi: 306.84'23-dc22

The Oprah Winfrey Show. (2006, January 1). *Let's talk about sex*. http://www. oprah.com/relationships/Lets-Talk-About-Sex/11

Weingarten, K. (2005). Reflections on families in the war zone: Narratives of "me" and the "other" in the course of therapy. In J. Kliman (Ed.) *Touched by the war zones, near and far: Oscillations of despair and hope* (pp. 26–28). Washington, DC: American Family Therapy Academy.

Weitzman, G. (2007). Counseling bisexuals in polyamorous relationships. In B. A. Firestein (Ed.) *Becoming Visible: Counseling bisexuals across the lifespan* (pp. 312–334). New York, NY: Columbia University Press.

MIX
Papier aus verantwortungsvollen Quellen
Paper from responsible sources
FSC® C105338

If you have any concerns about our products,
you can contact us on
ProductSafety@springernature.com

In case Publisher is established outside the EU,
the EU authorized representative is:
Springer Nature Customer Service Center GmbH
Europaplatz 3, 69115 Heidelberg, Germany

Printed by Libri Plureos GmbH
in Hamburg, Germany